The Fundrai Irresistible C ....unications

Real-World, Field-Tested Strategies
for Raising More Money

Also by Emerson & Church

How to Write Fundraising Materials that Raise More Money, by Tom Ahern, 187 pp., $24.95.

Whenever we're called upon to draft a solicitation letter, or write copy for the website, or, heaven forbid, pen long stretches of a proposal or case statement, we sit there … and if we're lucky crank out serviceable prose. Few would call it sparkling. Even fewer are moved to write a check in response.

It won't be this way any longer for those who invest a few hours in *How to Write Fundraising Materials that Raise More Money*. Communicating with donors is the bedrock of all fundraising. And no book addresses this topic with such virtuosity.

Seeing Through a Donor's Eyes, by Tom Ahern, 167 pp., $24.95.

Successful donor newsletters, websites, annual reports, donor acquistion programs, email, direct mail, and, yes, capital campaigns, too, all have one thing in common: behind each stands a well-reasoned, emotionally satisfying case for support.

Regularly reviewing your case is mere due diligence in a well-managed fundraising office. And it doesn't have to be a laborious project, either: answer three questions and you can be done.

Of course, if your office is launching a big-bucks campaign, the step-by-step process revealed in this book guarantees you'll tell a persuasive, sharply focused story, even when you have a thousand moving parts.

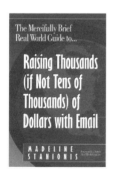

Raising Thousands (if Not Tens of Thousands) of Dollars with Email, by Madeline Stanionis, 108 pp., $24.95.

After reading the title of this book, you're saying: "Sure, Red Cross and Salvation Army can raise tons of money with email, but my agency isn't a brand name. You're telling me I can do the same!?"

Not of the same scale, no. But what Madeline Stanionis is saying is that you can raise a healthy amount if you approach email fundraising with a measure of intelligence and creativity.

Stanionis reveals precisely what you need to do, step by step, to raise substantial money with email.

www.emersonandchurch.com

THE

FUNDRAISER'S GUIDE
to Irresistible Communications

Real-World Field-Tested Strategies for Raising More MONEY

Jeff Brooks

Emerson
& Church
PUBLISHERS

www.emersonandchurch.com

First printed in September 2012

10 9 8 7 6 5 4 3 2

Printed in the United States of America

This text is printed on acid-free paper.

Copies of this book are available from the publisher at discount when purchased in quantity for boards of directors or staff.

Emerson & Church, Publishers
15 Brook Street * Medfield, MA 02052
Tel. 508-359-0019 * Fax 508-359-2703
www.emersonandchurch.com

Library of Congress Cataloging-in-Publication Data
Brooks, Jeff, 1961–
    The fundraiser's guide to irresistible communications : real-world, field-tested strategies for raising more money / Jeff Brooks.
        p.   cm.
    ISBN 978-1-889102-02-3 (pbk. : alk. paper)   1. Fund raising.
2. Nonprofit organizations—Marketing.   3. Nonprofit organizations—
Public relations.   I. Title.
HV41.2.B76 2012
658.15'224--dc23

Contents

PART I

The Writing Style of Fundraising

There's a new sheriff in town. The development department has been taken over by someone with deep experience in commercial marketing. She helped sell millions of dollars of breakfast cereal. Or was it software? Whichever it was, she's smart and experienced, a real change agent. Everyone's excited about the changes she'll bring.

One of the first acts the new director takes is an audit of the fundraising program. Her findings are harsh. "Our messaging isn't creative. It's outdated. It lacks a clear brand."

Word goes out: overhaul everything!

So everything changes. Spiffy new logo! Flashy modern fonts! Up-to-date colors! Pedestrian old fundraising offers are replaced with a high-flown "brand promise." Celebrities are recruited to star in amusing YouTube videos extolling the merits of the organization.

Then revenue drops. And drops. And then plummets.

The new boss quietly resigns and returns to her former field, where she'll happily sell software (cereal?) for the rest of her career. It takes about a year for the organization to correct course and recapture the revenue it was generating before the changes.

I've watched this scenario play out again and again. It happens almost every time someone from outside the field decides to ignore what's known about fundraising.

The moral of the story is this: Fundraising is a profession. It has a body of knowledge and a set of principles. It's not a jerry-rigged monstrosity created by amateurs and volunteers. It's not a dumbed-down version of commercial marketing.

A lot of us in the field—just about everyone—did something else before we became fundraisers. And that means nearly every one of us has a learning curve. Especially when it comes to communication and writing.

The writing style of fundraising is different. It can be a bit of a shock. If your experience is in standard business writing, you may find it too casual, too personal, and too urgent.

If you learned how to write in journalism classes, you may find fundraising subjective, sensationalistic, and repetitive.

If your background is academic, you may find fundraising messy, emotional, and simplistic.

If you come from commercial advertising, you may find fundraising dull and old-fashioned.

The strange conventions of fundraising are the result of decades of experience, discipline, and head-to-head testing. It shows us what works and what doesn't.

This ability to test is a huge advantage. Writers in most other writing disciplines are pretty much in the dark about their real effectiveness. When a journalist writes an article, how does he know it accomplished its purpose of clearly and accurately conveying information? He relies on his own judgment, based on his training and experience. He receives comments from an editor. Once the article goes public, comments from readers may give some sense of whether he hit the mark.

But really, a journalist can only estimate success. He never learns exactly how many readers understood, or how well.

In fundraising, we know *exactly* how many donors respond to our messages. We know how much each one gave. We know how many gave again—and how much and how often. With email we know even more, like how many opened our messages and how many clicked through to the website but still didn't give.

When those numbers aren't good, we know we have to change something.

Everything in the next few chapters is based on testing and experience. Some of the conventions I'll discuss will annoy you—heck, they annoy *me*. I'd change them if I could. But my responsibility, and yours, is to raise money for good causes. Neither you nor I have the right to impose our tastes or preferences at the expense of raising funds.

I hope to help you understand—and maybe even enjoy— the unique style of fundraising writing. Once you get past disliking or disbelieving the conventions, you can move on to the better, deeper joy of generating more revenue for life-enriching causes.

CHAPTER 1

The Importance of Being Urgent

Man down! It looks like a heart attack. You spring into action, knowing a life may be at stake.

If you've had CPR training, you know that one of the first things to do is pick a bystander, point at him, and loudly say, "You—call 9-1-1!"

Why not shout, "Somebody call 9-1-1"? After all, anyone can call. But the training makes it clear: You put all the pressure on one person. If you don't, it's possible (in fact, likely) that every single bystander will think, "Someone else will do it"—and nobody will make the lifesaving call.

Fundraising requires that same sense of aggressive urgency. When it's not there, when it's the equivalent of "Somebody call 9-1-1!" we get the same result. Everyone thinks someone else will take care of it. Hardly anyone gives.

Think about it from the donor's point of view. When your fundraising message shows up, it's out of the blue. She's doing something else, not waiting to hear from you. She's predisposed *not* to take action.

Most donors won't give unless they have a reason to give NOW. They'll move on to something demanding their attention. The phone is ringing. The dog needs a walk. Or there's an urgent request from another organization needing money *now*.

You'll only secure a gift if you help the donor move from a state of inaction to one of action. And you do that by putting the three ingredients of urgency to work:

1. Your call to action requires *immediate* action. Not think about it and respond eventually. Not become generally predisposed to agree with the cause. Respond. Now.

2. Your message clearly communicates what's at stake— that is, what's likely to happen if the donor doesn't give.

3. You're talking to *one person*. Even when using a mass medium like television, your message points a finger at one bystander and says, "You—give now!"

Let's look at each of these ingredients.

1. Immediate action

Urgency should never be a "technique" you tack on to your message, like offering a clever premium or using an attention-grabbing font. It must always be real, a genuine response to the situation, the way it is when you're kneeling next to a heart-attack victim.

You can pinpoint that urgency by asking yourself, "Why should we take action today, rather than wait three months?" You'll come up with answers like the following:

- ▶ People may not survive if we don't help them quickly. (*Food has run out in the refugee camp, and every day the children move closer to starving.*)
- ▶ A window of opportunity will close. (*The historic building will be torn down if we don't raise the funds in time to renovate it.*)
- ▶ Conditions are going to change. (*A new law is about to take effect that will make our response impossible.*)

Scarcity is another source of urgency. There are situations where the donor will miss an opportunity if he delays:

- ▶ Matching funds. (*Only the first $50,000 raised can be matched, so give now to make sure your gift is doubled.*)
- ▶ The opportunity is limited. (*The endangered wetland is 100 acres. Hurry to save one of those precious acres.*) Or even (*There are only 250 tiles in the lobby where we can display donors' names.*)

Lastly, you can increase the urgency and make it more specific with a deadline (one of the most effective fundraising deadlines is December 31).

Deadlines work best when they're connected with something real. (*School is out on June 15. That's when we need to start providing lunches for needy kids.*) But even an arbitrary deadline can move donors to give rather than put it off.

2. What's at stake

When someone collapses on the sidewalk, it's clear what's at stake: It's literally a life-or-death situation that requires action. You can't count on that level of clarity when you're raising funds. Donors have little idea what's at stake until you tell them their gift is *important*—and that *not* giving will have terrible consequences. Make the stakes clear:

> ▶ *If we don't save this land, it'll be lost to sprawl forever. Our children and grandchildren will never stand in the cathedral-like forest or hear the call of the ravens there.*
> ▶ *Please help move Alzheimer's research forward. Chances are someone you love—maybe even you yourself—will someday face this disease. Your gift now will help shape what treatment will be available when you need it!*
> ▶ *Winter is just around the corner. Your gift now will help a homeless person get off the street before the weather turns deadly.*

3. One person at a time

From your position as a fundraiser, you can see the big picture. You ask a lot of people to give, and, realistically, you and your organization will be fine if just 5 percent of your donors contribute. But taking this view lulls you into a false sense of security. Think this way, and you'll engage in non-urgent, ineffective fundraising.

You have to aim for *100 percent response* every time. Put every single donor on the line. That's the only way to get the 5 percent you need. If you communicate like you're trying for 5 percent, you'll get something closer to 1 percent.

One of the main reasons donors don't give is this: *They think their gifts don't matter.* "My $25 is too small to make a difference. Why bother?"

When donors think that way, it's *our fault.* We aren't communicating enough urgency. We've failed to show that each gift—even if the donor thinks it's small—is critical, is needed right away, and *makes a difference.* Donors need to clearly hear statements such as:

- ▶ Your gift will feed a hungry person.
- ▶ Your gift will keep baby seals from being clubbed to death.
- ▶ Your gift will keep the life-transforming power of theater strong in the young people of our community.
- ▶ Your gift will bring us that much closer to a cure for cancer.

The common non-urgent approach is to say something like "Your gift will fund our ongoing work." This makes an individual gift seem small and unimportant. And it lacks emotional punch. No wonder so many organizations struggle to raise funds!

When donors receive urgent fundraising messages, they know they have a role in making the world a better place. They get excited about how much their gift matters. They know they must respond now—and they *want* to respond now!

When your donors get this message, you've done your job. You're a certified fundraiser.

CHAPTER 2

Make It Easy to Read

If you've ever had the singular misfortune of being assigned a required reading list that included any books by the French philosopher Jacques Derrida, please accept my condolences, because no doubt you've struggled mightily to read—much less comprehend—Mr. Derrida's philosophical prose, which generally gets an astonishingly high reading-ease level of around 20th grade.

Excuse me. That was hard to read. I'm sorry. The reading-ease grade level of that paragraph is 19. Almost as high as Derrida! A lot of folks wouldn't make it through prose like that. This paragraph is easier. Its reading-ease grade level is 4.

There's an important difference between the grade 19 of the first paragraph and the grade 4 of the second. In fundraising, that difference can spell success or failure.

What makes copy easy to read are *short sentences* and *short words*. It doesn't have run-on sentences that connect thought after thought without a pause (think Marcel Proust or William Faulkner). It uses few multisyllabic words such as *multisyllabic*. If readers have to labor to read your fundraising message, they usually won't bother. They'll stop reading. If they don't read it, they aren't likely to respond.

This isn't because donors are ignorant or inattentive. It's because concentration is hard work, and most people are already doing all the mental work they care to do. You have to earn every second of their attention, and one of the best ways is to make what you write easy to read.

The most common reading-ease tool is the Flesch-Kincaid Grade Level. It's a standard that looks at sentence length and the number of long words to yield a grade level. Microsoft Word calculates the grade level as part of its grammar-check function. You can also find online calculators. Google "Flesch Kincaid."

Effective fundraising copy has a reading-ease level somewhere between 4th and 6th grade.

Above 6th-grade level, it takes more concentration to read. The reader has to slow down. If she's in a hurry, she'll skim—or give up.

If copy is above 12th-grade level, it's a flat-out struggle. Few readers will bother unless they're forced to. Like the poor saps with Derrida in their required reading.

Some fundraisers actually try to keep their writing at a high grade level. They're working under the mistaken assumption that grade level means education level. They believe if they're writing for an audience that's college educated, the copy will be inappropriate unless it's at 13th-grade level or higher.

That misguided notion leads to a lot of copy that nobody reads. Don't let that happen to your fundraising!

Here's one of the most important truths I can tell you: Reading ease is *not about education*. And it's especially *not about intelligence*.

Sixth-grade level copy isn't just for 6th-graders. It's just easier to read. Easier for everyone, no matter how well educated.

Think of low-grade-level writing as a form of courtesy. It's like enunciating clearly when you speak. Or using neat handwriting. Even the most intellectual PhD will appreciate and respond to clear communication.

In fact, the most highly educated people are often the busiest. They're fully capable of reading difficult prose, but if you write to them in clear, easy language they can read it faster and get the point more quickly. Can you think of a smart, educated, busy person who doesn't want things to be quick and easy?

Writing at a low grade level is actually hard. Your first draft is too high—mine always is. The good news is, the way to fix it is straightforward. Just concentrate on two things:

1. **Keep sentences short.** Any sentence over thirty words is a candidate for splitting into two (or more) shorter sentences. Don't be afraid to use sentence fragments. Even one- and two-word sentences.

   Not all long sentences can be chopped in two; the pieces won't be graceful or coherent. These are the ones you have to rethink and rewrite.

2. **Purge the big words.** Every time you find a word that's three or more syllables, ask yourself: Is there a short word that'll work instead? Use *help* instead of *assistance*. *Cause* instead of *necessitate*. *Use* instead of *utilize*.

You don't need to remove all of the long words. (In most cases, *intestines* is more appropriate than *guts*.) But the fewer long words there are, the easier your message will be to read.

It is possible for the grade level to be too low. At 3rd-grade level or lower, copy can have a choppy, disjointed sound, like a children's book. *Dick can run. See Dick run. Run, Dick, run!* The best writers can pull it off, writing at extremely low grade level without sounding silly. Ernest Hemingway's writing topped out at about 4th grade. Not too many would accuse Hemingway of sounding childish.

But the rest of us? Stay between 4th- and 6th-grade level.

CHAPTER 3

Long Messages Work Better

Aunt Ruth was smiling. Aglow with happiness. I couldn't figure it out.

My 79-year-old aunt had just brought in the day's mail. There was a lot of it, including several fundraising appeals. She threw one away unopened. The others she set on the small table next to her comfy chair. Smiling. The whole time.

"I'm going to read my mail now," she said in the same tone someone would say, "I'm going skiing this weekend."

Suddenly it came to me: Aunt Ruth *likes reading her mail.* Even the "junk mail." To Aunt Ruth, those unsolicited letters aren't an annoying fundraising tactic—they're a connection to people she's interested in and causes she cares about.

One time Aunt Ruth called to tell me something she'd read in an appeal: "Did you know it only costs twelve cents to keep a little boy or girl from going blind? Twelve cents!" That wasn't a clever marketing proposition to Aunt Ruth—it was an exciting piece of news. A relevant fact worth sharing.

Aunt Ruth is a reader. Her love of mail may strike you as bizarre, but it's common among donors.

Every fundraiser needs an Aunt Ruth. She can keep your mind open to different ways of thinking, including the radical notion that many donors *love to hear from us.*

That love of reading what the postman brings helps explain why direct mail is such a powerful fundraising medium. It dwarfs the next runner-up, which is the telephone. It also sheds light on an even greater mystery: why longer messages usually work better at raising funds than short ones.

I hate long letters. I wish they'd just get to the point. I bet *you* don't care for long letters either. Nevertheless, long messages *work.*

I've tested long against short many times. In direct mail, the shorter message only does better about 10 percent of the time (a short message does tend to work better for emergency fundraising).

But most often, if you're looking for a way to improve an appeal, add another page. Most likely it'll boost response. Often it can generate a higher average gift too.

It's true in email as well, though not as decisively so. In my experience, a longer email outperforms a shorter one about two out of three times. Brevity may be a virtue in the emails you write to coworkers, but longer emails still get through to a lot of donors.

In surveys and focus groups, donors often complain about long fundraising messages. They say exactly what you or I would say: "I don't have time to read something that long. Why don't they get to the point?"

That's what they *say*. But in real life, donors respond more often to long messages. We don't know why, but here are some theories:

> ▶ *The Aunt Ruth Theory:* Many donors just enjoy reading. More words mean more reading pleasure, and that means more connection and increased chances a person will give.

> ▶ *The Multiple Triggers Theory:* Some donors are likely to give when you help them visualize a life-threatening need. Others will be moved if you emphasize a great deal. The longer the message, the more triggers you can include.

> ▶ *The Hopscotch Theory:* Few people read everything you've written, starting with the first word and ending with the last. Just watch someone, anyone, while they read their mail. They start where their eyes land. They bounce around, leaping forward and backward, skipping entire sections, reading other parts more than once. I once watched my mother read an appeal I'd written (she didn't know it was mine). She started at the end and worked her way backward. The last sentence she read was my carefully crafted lead. A longer letter has more

entry points. More calls to action. More chances for a reader who isn't following your logic to get pulled in.

▶ *The Gravitas Theory:* The very fact that a message is long may signal to donors in some subliminal way that it's important. They may not need to read every word, because the length tells them all they need to know.

I've found that the best long messages have two characteristics: *repetition* and *story.*

Repetition is the important part. Repeat yourself because you don't know if readers understood what you said the first time. Repeat yourself because you can't be sure they caught it the first and second times. Repeat yourself because sometimes it doesn't sink in until you've said it a few times. Repeat yourself because you never know what way of making the case is the one that will get through.

The outline for an effective long fundraising message might be something like this:

▶ Introduction: Why I'm writing to you.
▶ Ask.
▶ Why your gift is so important today.
▶ Ask.
▶ How much impact your gift will have.
▶ Ask.
▶ Story that demonstrates the need.
▶ Ask.
▶ Remind the donor of his values and connection with the cause.

- ► Ask.
- ► Another story.
- ► Ask.
- ► Help the donor visualize what will happen when she gives.
- ► Ask.
- ► Conclusion: Thank the donor for caring. Ask again.

You may think I'm exaggerating. I'm not. If you're serious about raising funds, you really have to ask, again and again.

Stories can shine in a longer message. The difference between a richly detailed story and one that's been pared down to fit in a small space can be like the difference between a snapshot and a film. For example, here's how you might write about the cruel practice of bear baiting if you're writing a short message:

The bear sat on its haunches, bleeding from its injured mouth.

The longer version is more vivid:

The bear sat on its haunches, rocking back and forth, blood pooling in the dirt beneath it. One side of its mouth was torn open and hanging loose, exposing the teeth and drizzling saliva and blood into its matted fur.

The reality quotient, the sense that the reader has actually witnessed the scene, is higher in the long version. And when the reader has a vivid experience with your cause—even when it's only through the written word—she's much more likely to give.

Some people believe the era of long messages is ending. They say text messaging, 140-character tweets, and changes in the ways people communicate and retrieve information work against people sitting down to read the way Aunt Ruth does. Maybe. But so far, longer messages are holding their own.

The important thing is this: You can't judge this issue by what you'd want in your own mailbox. You can't even base it on what donors tell you they want. You have to watch *actual donor behavior* as it plays out in the form of response to your messages.

So until you learn otherwise, keep sending those long messages. Aunt Ruth will certainly thank you.

CHAPTER 4

Grammar for Fundraisers

D r. Abe was an intelligent, learned man. A respected theologian, he'd authored several books, including a noteworthy volume on prayer. Not a book you or I would read if we wanted to learn how to pray, but a tome on the theory of prayer.

When it came to writing, Dr. Abe had chops. He had a rich, elegant style—it often sounded like the Declaration of Independence. He was justly proud of his way with words.

Dr. Abe led a nonprofit, and he attacked the job of writing fundraising appeals with zeal. His letters were long (which you know is good). But that's not all: his letters were logical. They were impeccably correct. Packed with knowledge and interesting allusions.

And they didn't work.

In fact, Dr. Abe's fundraising results were so consistently bad his organization was spiraling toward total financial collapse.

Dr. Abe was making a common mistake. He thought good writing was good writing. He believed the style he used so effectively in his scholarly books was also the right style for fundraising appeals.

What Dr. Abe was missing was the vast difference in context between his books and his fundraising. The books are aimed at committed readers who clear the decks, get comfortable, and are ready to concentrate. Who fully expect to stop and think and to absorb what they're reading. Who respect and enjoy writing that showcases an educated and subtle mind.

Fundraising? It's aimed at readers who are doing something else. Who have no commitment whatsoever to wrestling with a message. Who, if they aren't moved to action right away, will abandon the message without a second thought.

These two audiences might as well speak different languages.

Funny thing is, those book readers and fundraising readers are usually the same people. Someone could step away from the rigor of reading a scholarly book and become a short-attention-span fundraising reader without missing a beat. Context is everything.

If Dr. Abe wrote a book the way fundraising is written, his publisher would think he'd gone loony. His theologian buddies would laugh him right out of the faculty lounge at the seminary.

But that's exactly the mistake he was making when he wrote fundraising messages the way he wrote his books. Except nobody was laughing. They were just ignoring his attempts to raise money for a great cause.

Fundraising copy that works is colloquial, informal, and simple. It doesn't call attention to the education of the writer. In fact, it's far more important to sound natural than it is to obey the grammar, usage, and structure rules your English teachers taught you.

Let me admit something here: before I was a fundraiser, I *was* an English teacher. I taught the rules of grammar and composition to thousands of students. I struggled and sweated to make them understand and value good academic writing.

And I wrote a lot like Dr. Abe (though he's better than I was).

Then I became a fundraiser. Like many who have an academic background, I struggled. My best writing wasn't getting the job done. The better I wrote, the worse the results.

But I couldn't see the pattern.

It came to me suddenly one day. I was reading some of my own copy, enjoying an especially elegant turn of phrase, mentally patting myself on the back for my cleverness. Then, out of the blue, I had a vision of my mother reading that same passage. It became clear that my beautiful writing would have puzzled and annoyed her. I could visualize her frown as she made a good-faith attempt to understand what I'd written.

Mom was no slouch. She was college educated (master's degree, in fact), and fully capable of understanding high-toned writing.

But she would have said, "Jeffrey" (she was the only one who called me that), "if you want me to give, why don't you just say so?"

I immediately embarked on a self-imposed reeducation program to become a real fundraising writer. Changing your writing style isn't easy. But if you know what you're aiming for, anyone can do it.

Here are some of the principles I discovered about fundraising copy:

▶ Paragraphs don't have to start with a topic sentence. And they don't have to contain one complete idea. In fundraising, the paragraph isn't a unit of information. It's a visual structure.

▶ Sentence fragments? No problem. Fragments add energy to copy and improve reading ease.

▶ And feel free to start sentences with conjunctions. They help propel the reader forward.

▶ Contractions are a must. If you do not use them, you will sound like a robot.

▶ Footnotes should be banned from fundraising copy. A footnote is like a neon sign that says NOT PERSONAL. If you need to provide a source for something, do it in a colloquial way. (Instead of following a fact with a footnote, say, "I know this because I read it in last April's edition of the *Journal of Important Facts*, on page 36, if you want to look it up.")

▶ Semicolons, the lawyer's favorite punctuation mark, should be avoided. They're formal and legalistic. Hardly anyone knows how to use them correctly, so they're confusing for many readers. If you know how to use semicolons, congratulations; just don't use them in fundraising.

▶ Any grammar rule that people don't commonly use in speech is a candidate for ignoring. Correct use of "whom" doesn't sound natural to most people. Write sentences to avoid using it. Or, if you're daring, just say "who" instead of "whom."

▶ Don't make an allusion unless you're confident everyone will get it. You can say, "Our office is like a Santa's workshop of activity." Any American will know what that means. But if you said, "He was as gentle and wise as Elder Zosima," you'd impress the heck out of *me*, but you'd lose almost everyone else, even those who've read *The Brothers Karamazov*.

▶ Avoid puns and wordplay. They're much loved by writers, but most people don't get them, don't care, and find them confusing or annoying.

▶ And here's something that's going to be a knife in the heart of former English majors: use clichés. There's a reason clichés catch on. They express things people often want to express—in short (and sweet) ways that are easy (as pie) to remember.

There's also a set of silly rules you should ignore. These rules have no purpose other than to separate people who went to college from those who didn't. They include:

- ▶ Don't end sentences with prepositions.
- ▶ Avoid split infinitives.
- ▶ Never use exclamation marks outside of direct quotes.

Rules like these serve no useful purpose in fundraising.

If you have a copy of *The Elements of Style* by Strunk and White, disregard everything it says. This little book is widely admired in English departments, and many people swear by it. The problem is, most of its rules and advice will lead to stilted, formal prose that'll hurt your fundraising results.

I'm not saying you should be sloppy. Know your *its* from your *it's* and your *their* from your *there*. Spell words correctly. Make sure every sentence connects with those around it. Messy, graceless, error-filled copy can turn away readers as quickly as over-formal, too-academic copy.

Just don't write to show off your degrees or your IQ. Write to touch people's hearts and move them to action.

By the way, Dr. Abe eventually mastered the fundraising style. He didn't enjoy it much, but he bit the bullet and did it because he cared a lot more about funding his cause than about his personal writing style.

If Dr. Abe could do it, and I could do it, anyone who wants to can learn the fundraising way of writing.

PART II

The Content of Fundraising

Most languages have a quirk English doesn't have: nouns have gender. In Spanish, "eyebrow" is feminine. "Eye" is masculine. Go figure.

It's called grammatical gender. Typically, there are masculine, feminine, and sometimes neuter nouns. Some languages have ten or even more "genders." (*That* would be fun to learn.)

If you're a native English speaker and you've studied another language, chances are grammatical gender drove you crazy. It's hard to remember. You're always getting it wrong. Anyway, we do fine without it in English.

But if you speak a language that has grammatical gender, you know it has purpose. It adds beauty and structure to the language. It's used with skill by poets. There are even jokes built around getting it wrong.

In the next few chapters, I'm going to show you some of the grammar of fundraising. Some of it may seem weird. It may even annoy you, or seem just plain stupid. Either way, I'll show you some of the things that make fundraising work, such as:

- ▶ Why facts and statistics can turn away donors.
- ▶ Why simplicity is king in fundraising, even in our complex world.
- ▶ Why we talk about the donor instead of the projects we're raising money for.
- ▶ What a good fundraising message has in common with an old "I've got good news and bad news" joke.
- ▶ Why fundraising should be straightforward, no matter how uncomfortable it makes you.
- ▶ Why you include a P.S. with your fundraising message . . . including your email.

These fundraising conventions aren't carved-in-stone commandments to obey at all costs. They're principles, and there are times when departing from them is the right thing to do. But the professionals think twice before doing that. Simply disliking one of these conventions is the worst possible reason for ignoring it!

CHAPTER 5

Persuade with Story, Not Statistics

*K*aramojong!

That's probably a meaningless word to you. But when I heard Benny mutter it under his breath, it was the most terrifying word I'd ever heard.

I was in northern Uganda, gathering stories for a client that worked in impoverished communities there. Benny, a muscular young man who laughed easily, was my driver. We'd spent several days going from one village to the next for interviews.

Something was wrong, oddly out of place, in these villages. I couldn't put my finger on it until Benny mentioned it: there were no cows. Not one.

If you've seen Africa only on television, you might think it's all elephants, lions, and other zoo animals. It's not. You have to go far out of your way to see those. The iconic animals of Africa are cattle. Long-horned, sleepy-eyed cattle. They're everywhere.

But not here in northern Uganda. All the cattle had been stolen. In interview after interview, people told me about the raids of the Karamojong, a neighboring tribal people.

Like many herding cultures around the world, the Karamojong believe that cattle—all cattle—are created by God expressly for them. Taking cattle from others isn't stealing; it's restoring them to their rightful owners.

A long drought had plunged the Karamojong into famine. Their children were starving. Desperate, they swarmed into the lowlands, armed with rifles and machetes, to take the cattle they saw as their own. Some of the raids were violent: they burned houses, even killed a number of villagers. Nearly everyone I met had a terrifying personal story of a Karamojong raid.

On the last evening of my visit, as we drove in the smoky dusk, a truck loomed out of the darkness and barreled down the highway toward us. It was covered with people, standing shoulder-to-shoulder in the back, even hanging off the sides. We could hear them chanting over the roar of the engine.

Benny gripped his steering wheel. He wasn't laughing. "Karamojong," he said. "Hide your face."

I covered my white face and prayed. The truck bore down on us. An incoherent scene played out in my mind. Gunshots. Angry faces. Me, bound and blindfolded and kept in an airless room while they figured out whether I was worth keeping alive as a hostage.

Then the truck roared past. As it did, we saw that there were as many women as men on the truck, and we saw no guns.

They were local people, not Karamojong raiders. They were likely on their way to a wedding, singing.

I'd been writing about Africa for years. I knew about the conflict between farming and herding cultures that goes back to prehistoric times. I knew how drought, poverty, and too many guns make the clash more violent. It's the background of the tragedy in Darfur, a few hundred miles to the north. It's the same force that brought down the Roman Empire.

But that conflict was just an idea, a fact with no impact—like the price of a shirt you'll never buy—until a truckload of armed cattle raiders was aimed straight at me. Or so I thought.

What had been an abstract idea became gut-wrenching reality in that minute. Now I know what the herder/farmer conflict means, how it *feels*—in the pit of the stomach, in the sweat running down your neck, in rushed, broken prayers for survival.

I don't just know. I feel and understand.

And you do too. Because I've told you this story. Story, not facts.

We're all tempted to marshal facts and send them out like an army to battle people into being generous. That doesn't work. If you want people to give, you have to touch them deeply. And to do that, you must tell stories. The human mind isn't moved by facts. We forget facts. We fail to internalize them. We miss their meaning and importance.

But stories help us make sense of the world. Stories move us to action.

So many fundraisers think the size or intractability of a problem is what makes it compelling. What they're missing is that donors don't want to solve a problem because it's big. They want to solve it because it's *solvable*.

You've heard that 22,000 children die from hunger-related causes every day. That's mind-boggling. Heartbreaking.

I spent years looking for ways to make that fact vivid. I talked about how many children die in an hour (917) or a minute (15; that's one every four seconds). I painted visions of emptied-out American towns with populations of around 22,000 (Portsmouth, New Hampshire, or Fairfax, Virginia).

It never worked.

The fundraising that works is always about a sick baby. Or a father who couldn't grow enough food for his family. Stories.

The fact that the daily death toll is mind-boggling is exactly why it's a terrible fundraising platform. It's a fact we can't process. It has so many human faces it effectively has no face at all.

If you want action, you must help donors feel the pain of hunger by seeing it play out in one life. Then give them the opportunity to save *one life*—then another and another. That's how you'll get them working with you to solve big problems.

It's one pelican, covered in sticky tar and flopping along the beach, that galvanizes response to an oil spill. Not the reports of millions of gallons of oil churning into the ocean.

It's a Parkinson's disease patient, struggling with shaking hands to button a button. Not the fact that 1 percent of people over age sixty suffer from Parkinson's.

Massive natural disasters may seem to be an exception to the principle that big numbers don't make good fundraising. Disasters like the 2004 Indian Ocean tsunami and the 2010 Haiti earthquake have stirred outpourings of charitable giving. The bigger the disaster, the greater the response.

But it's not the numbers that motivate people to give.

When a disaster is big—and big is measured by number of deaths—the news media send swarms of reporters. For a while, videos, photos, and stories from the disaster zone are inescapable.

We all see the man clinging to the roof of a car as it spins in the black water of the tsunami. Or the baby wailing alone in the rubble of the earthquake.

These news accounts and video clips are the stories that motivate us to give. The painful truth is that it takes massive death tolls to get the news media telling the story.

Most of the time, the media won't show up to cover the tragedies we care about. It's up to us to tell the stories that will inspire donors to give. An effective fundraising story usually has these elements going for it:

> ▶ It's an account of *one person* (or a very few people). If the story is about world hunger or the education crisis, it's not a real story. A few years ago, *New York Times* columnist Nicholas Kristof theorized that if there were an endangered puppy in Darfur, Americans would pay attention to the crisis. He was right. One living thing—

even when it's not a human—can capture people's attention.

- It has *conflict*. Something isn't right. Food has run out. The salmon can't get past the dam to their spawning place. A talented kid can't afford to go to college. Every meaningful story is about something that's broken.

- It has *details*. The reader can picture the situation, see the faces, hear the sounds. Maybe even taste, touch, and feel. Sensory details make the story more memorable and help it reach deep into our emotions.

- It's *well written*. It has strong verbs and concrete nouns. It's easy to read and has a pleasing rhythm. Of course, all your fundraising copy, not just the stories, should be well written. But a story needs to be written at a higher level.

- It has a *fundraising ending*. That is, it's not quite finished. Malaria is endemic in the village. Children are dying and their parents are unable to work. Bed nets would solve the problem—but *the bed nets are not yet distributed*. A fundraising story that ends with a fully resolved problem makes it clear that the donor isn't needed.

A good fundraising story shouldn't read like a novel, with poetic descriptions and narrative alternating with dialog. In fact, if your story reads more like a book than like a person talking, it calls attention to itself and pulls the focus away from the call to action. And that defeats the purpose of the story in the first place.

You can tell a story in as few as two or three sentences, with a vivid "word picture" that captures the situation you want your donor to see:

> The young mom hugs her baby tight to her chest. She has no milk for him—hasn't for several days. The baby isn't crying, but that's bad news: he's simply too weak from hunger to cry.

*   *   *

And now I think you're ready for the real inside scoop about fundraising storytelling, the principle that sets it apart from other types of storytelling, that's known only by true black-belt practitioners: the best story of all is the story where *the donor is the hero.*

In most stories, the audience is on the outside, looking in. We see Odysseus clinging to the underside of a sheep while he escapes the blinded Cyclops. We watch as Ripley blows the alien out of her spaceship. We may identify with these heroes, but they're not us.

In the best fundraising stories, the audience, the donor, is inside the story. You never go too many sentences without shining the spotlight back on the donor. You make it clear she has the power, the will, and the compassion to make the world a better place by giving.

Whether your story is about a starving child in the middle of Africa or an actor who's working to break the hearts and transform the minds of an audience—you keep returning to the donor and how he's connected to the powerful, world-changing drama. Make it clear the donor is the hero.

You can do that by directly addressing the donor, saying things like:

- You're one of those special people who understands and cares about this cause.
- This is a great opportunity, because your generosity will stretch even further than usual.
- The children will have you to thank—for saving and transforming their lives.

Some organizations struggle with the concept of the donor as hero. They're so aware of the hard and sometimes sacrificial work being done by their staffs, they see the donor in a supporting role—barely a sidekick to the real heroes. All the donor does is write a check now and then. The staff give their hearts, souls, and sweat every day. A nonprofit insider once told me that too much focus on donors might make staff feel "marginalized" by comparison.

This kind of thinking makes two serious errors:

1. *Without donors, most nonprofit organizations wouldn't exist.* The staff's great work would never get out of the idea file if not for those checks from donors.

2. *The purpose of fundraising is to motivate donors to give.* Not to boost the morale of staff. How fundraising makes the staff feel isn't relevant. By all means make sure your

staff are getting the recognition they deserve. Just don't try to use your fundraising to do that.

* * *

A few pages ago, I told you a story about my non-encounter with Karamojong raiders in Africa. I wanted you to think about stories and experience how powerful they can be.

I also had another reason for telling you about the Karamojong. Remember how they believe all cattle belong to them?

Fundraisers should be that way about *stories*.

We own all the stories. God made stories so we could hear them. And tell them. And motivate people to give. It's a tribal belief we fundraisers carry in our heads and our guts. We are in fact the Karamojong of stories.

CHAPTER 6

Keep It Simple

A dusty, bearded Middle Eastern holy man stood up and told the story of a traveler who was attacked by robbers, left for dead, then rescued by an unexpected hero.

There wasn't much to the story: fewer than two hundred words when it was written down. But it covered a lot of ground. It was about the power of good deeds. Our duty toward fellow humans. Why we shouldn't be prejudiced. And a lot more.

You could build your life around that story. Many people have.

Today we know it as the Parable of the Good Samaritan. It's a masterpiece of making complex ideas simple, clear, and compelling.

Fundraising needs to be like that: clear, compelling, but most of all, simple.

Simplicity is a challenge for many of us. We've become experts in our causes, and we've mastered the complexity of our organizations' work. We know the shades of gray.

That's all fine. But bring that complexity to your fundraising, and you'll fail to motivate donors.

No matter how complex your organization's work, your fundraising must reduce it to a simple essence non-experts can understand. And understand quickly.

I once worked with a development director for an international relief organization. Let's call him "Rex." His background was working in Africa, but he'd contracted malaria and needed to stay stateside for a while. So they put him in charge of fundraising.

Working with Rex was good, because he knew what was happening in the field. You could walk up to him and say, "Northern Mozambique," and Rex would tell you all about conditions in the provinces of Niassa and Nampula. He seemed to know every village, every river—whether it was flooding or drying up—and how the sorghum, millet, and maize crops were coming along. I'd never been so well-equipped to tell donors what their gifts would do.

There was just one problem. Rex's favorite thing in the whole world was "civil society."

In case you're as little acquainted with the idea of civil society as I was, it's when there are reasonable laws, and people generally obey those laws and treat each other fairly. Corruption and violence are rare. Where civil society prevails, there's less hunger, more medical care, less crime, better business climate. Civil society is in fact a key part of the solution to most humanitarian problems.

That's why Rex always wanted to raise funds to encourage its spread. "Dude," he'd say, spreading his arms as if showing me the entire world. "You get so much bang for your buck with civil society!" He wanted to make it the focus of all our fundraising.

If you've been in fundraising for more than a few months, you won't be surprised to hear that our "civil society" appeals fell flat. But that didn't discourage Rex. He said we just needed to try harder, and we'd eventually find a way to motivate donors to support the idea. I didn't think so. I kept trying to raise funds to feed hungry children.

So Rex and I butted heads over and over again. Feed hungry children. Civil society. It was like one of those lite beer commercials.

Now, civil society is wonderful. No doubt about it. But it's not tangible. Most donors, most of the time, give to accomplish concrete goals. Like feeding hungry children. Concepts are nearly impossible to raise money for.

To successfully raise funds, you must go downstream from the concept until you're talking about concrete actions.

For example, a lot of organizations say their true goal is to spread *hope*.

But hope, as beautiful and inspiring as it is, is about as tangible as civil society. Hope is a powerful value—and sometimes an effective political slogan. But it's a weak fundraising proposition.

So even if your work spreads hope, you have to talk about the concrete actions that *lead to hope*: Helping farmers grow more crops. Resettling displaced families. Or feeding hungry children.

Maybe your mission is "Bolster the reproductive capacity of key cetacean species through habitat preservation." In fundraising, you need to say, "Save the whales."

Maybe the idea of your mission is "Reach out to underserved segments of the community with access to the musical masterworks of the 18th and 19th centuries, thereby building new audiences for serious music." In fundraising, you need to say, "Keep classical music alive."

It's not that donors are stupid. It's that they've spent a lot less time thinking about your cause than you have. Very few will ever become an expert like you—they have other things on their minds. But they can still wholeheartedly support your work—if you speak to *their* level of understanding, not yours.

Another way fundraising sometimes gets too complex is when it loses its focus. Successful fundraising is obsessively about one thing: give. Give now. Give to change the world in a very specific way.

It's tempting to make it "give plus" and throw in another goal or two. After all, you have other important objectives, and since you're going to all the trouble and expense of reaching out to supporters, why not kill two or more birds with one stone?

That's why some fundraisers confuse their donors with messages that add extra goals like these:

▶ "Think highly of us." It's easy to believe donors will give if they think well of you. But when you make this a goal, the message turns into self-centered bragging about your efficiency, your effectiveness, your history, and the education of your excellent staff. That's poor fundraising. It's great if donors think well of you, but that's not the point of fundraising. And really, they're more likely to think well of you after they give than before. Ask them to give.

▶ "Learn about our cause." You might think the right set of facts will educate people into giving. After all, knowing and understanding more about an issue can lead to a stronger connection to it, right? The problem is, education makes lousy fundraising. Donors give from the heart, and a lesson about your cause is unlikely to move many hearts. If you and your organization have a passion for educating people about your issue, think of it this way: people who give to a cause are far more open to becoming educated about it. Ask them to give. It's the best first lesson possible.

▶ "Change the way you think." That's the quick route to no response. Few people are able to change their thinking, and even fewer want to. And besides, a letter or email isn't an effective catalyst for changing attitudes. You won't change their thinking, and you won't get a gift. On the other hand, people who get involved with an issue by giving have a better chance of changing their thinking than those who don't. Ask them to give.

▶ "Talk to a planned giving officer." There's no question that involving donors in planned giving is worth doing. But when you try to accomplish two tasks in the same message, you end up doing neither. Ask them to give.

All these peripheral matters clutter the message and lower response.

When you need to communicate with donors about something other than giving, go to them with a separate message. And make that message about only one thing.

You're in the business of changing the world by raising funds. Don't stray from that. Just remember this fundraising checklist:

✔ Keep it simple.
✔ Keep it concrete.
✔ Ask, and do nothing else.

CHAPTER 7

Make It All About
the Donor

How many people do you know who drink Coke because they respect the Coca-Cola Company?

Probably none, unless you live in Atlanta.

People drink Coke because they like the way it tastes. Or, more likely, because it's on sale.

The Coca-Cola Company sells its product by appealing to people's inner reasons for buying Coke. They don't ask, "How can we make people think our company is great?" They ask, "What do people want, and how can we convince them we deliver that?"

I don't have inside knowledge about the Coca-Cola Company, but I'll bet some of the most important people there are chemists. (I imagine they're called something more impressive, like "flavor engineers.") Their job is to make sure Coke turns out right.

If the chemists didn't do their job and Coke started to taste like cod liver oil, the whole Coke premise would collapse. But they do their job. Coke tastes like Coke.

I can picture what happens every time there's a new marketing campaign for Coke: "It's the real thing," "Life begins here," "Coke is it."

Those poor chemists tear their hair out. "Are you kidding me?" they say. "These campaigns are so vague! So completely unconnected to our critical mission of keeping Coke within acceptable parameters."

But the marketing plugs along, stubbornly appealing to people's self-centered reasons.

And that's how you sell 1.6 billion Cokes every day.

I wish more nonprofits would think about their fundraising the way Coca-Cola thinks about marketing. Because they'd raise a lot more money and do a lot more good.

The best lesson you can draw from Coke's marketing is this: talk to donors where they are, not where you want them to be. Even if donors don't think the way you want them to think, their money is just as good as anyone else's. Actually, their money is better, because they give it away.

We as a profession are way behind the soft-drink industry in our understanding of customers. They've been working at it for a long time. They've spent billions on research. We may never catch up to their deep and practical knowledge.

But there's a lot we can do right now, with the knowledge and tools we have. The most important step is to learn from our relationships.

Your mother (or someone, I hope) told you that to get along with others, you should focus on *them*, not yourself. Right?

The worst way to make someone think you're cool is to tell them you're cool. In fact, telling people you're cool is generally proof that you're not cool at all. Like that guy who in every conversation mentions his membership in Mensa—everyone knows he's not exactly the brightest bulb in the chandelier.

It's the same in fundraising. Having a great reputation is a priceless asset. But the way to earn that reputation is by excelling for a long time—not by telling people how excellent you are. There's no shortcut around this reality.

Suppose you're the best cancer hospital in the region. Naturally, you'll be tempted to say, *We're the best cancer hospital in the region.* (And when you're marketing to potential patients, that's what you *should* say.)

But in fundraising, you need to put a donor twist on that fact. Something like, *Here's your opportunity to make meaningful progress in the fight against cancer.*

The basic statements you use to describe your work can become powerful fundraising propositions when you make them about donors:

- ▶ *We feed hungry people* should be *You feed hungry people.*
- ▶ *We are conquering asthma* should be *You are conquering asthma.*
- ▶ *We are building a strong ballet company in the Tri-City area* should be *You can build a strong ballet company in the Tri-City area.*

"We" statements invite no response. They have nothing to do with your donor, so there's little chance of stirring her to action. You're like an energetic four-year-old who keeps calling out, "Mommy, look at me! I have a bowl on my head! Daddy, look at me! I'm walking backwards!"

A four-year-old has an excuse: he hasn't yet learned that talking about himself isn't a good way to hold a conversation. A fundraiser can and should do better.

When you make a "you" statement, you hit the ball over to the donor's side of the court. You invite him to hit it back, to respond. He's compelled to interact, to at least say "yes" or "no." That's the first step to a donation. And even "no" is better than complete apathy.

What about your organization's long history, top-notch employees, and superior methodology? Do they even matter?

Yes. They matter immensely. You owe it to your mission—*and to your donors*—to be excellent in every way. But these factors *aren't the prime reasons donors give*. They're reasons they *continue* giving, or get involved in ways beyond giving.

There are some facts that help donors overcome the fear that you're running a scam. You should make them available to donors. Things like:

▶ Any ratings or approval from relevant watchdogs. These are very important for some donors.
▶ Third-party endorsements from experts, celebrities, the press, or other sources.
▶ Statements of openness and accountability.

These supporting elements are important, but they belong in secondary places in your fundraising messages: Pop-ups or sidebar links on the Web. The back of the reply coupon in direct mail. The "small print" elsewhere.

Facts about your organization and your work can be part of good fundraising, but only after you bring those facts into the donor's world—when you make them relevant, not self-focused bragging:

- ▶ Bragging: *We've been reaching out to the homeless in the community for 53 years.*
  Smart Fundraising: *Like you, we're part of this community. With the help of good neighbors like you, we've been feeding the homeless here since 1959.*
- ▶ Bragging: *Our way of distributing food is twice as efficient as anyone else's.*
  Smart Fundraising: *You'll stretch your dollars when you give, because we'll use your gift in an efficient way that gets twice as much food to the hungry for every dollar you give.*

The BOY Rule

Think about it this way. You're not raising money to fund your organization. You're enabling your donors to make the world a better place—*through* your organization.

That means the only facts that matter in fundraising are those you can directly connect to donors. To do that, apply the BOY Rule.

BOY stands for "Because Of You." It means you never lose a chance to credit donors for the good work your organization does. Make it a habit to include "Because Of You" with everything you say:

- ▶ Our programs help homeless people all over our city *Because Of You.*
- ▶ There are long stretches of beautiful open beaches and shoreline in our state *Because Of You.*
- ▶ New audience members enjoyed the ballet this year, including hundreds of elementary school kids *Because Of You.*

Sometimes you can't find a meaningful Because Of You. That's a clear sign you're just bragging. "Our president has written 17 books on all facets of Baltic folk dancing *Because Of You*" hardly works. Other facts aren't interesting to donors, like: "Our headquarters has electricity and running water *Because Of You*"—true, but not likely to capture anyone's heart.

An even better way to make your fundraising about donors is to praise them and appeal to their values.

You might think you don't know your donors well enough to do this in any meaningful way, but you do know two things about them: they've given, and they care about your cause. These are both significant facts that set your donors apart from ordinary people, and you present your cause accordingly:

You're a rare and well-informed person who understands North American crow and raven species and how important they are to our ecosystem and our way of life.

You can also compliment donors through what you have in common. Maybe they show Lutheran values, or have real Texas hospitality, or display the type of insight we can expect from State U grads.

It never hurts to note these points of connection. It can remind donors of their own virtues, and that makes them more likely to give.

Here's what's most important to remember. Post it on your wall. Tattoo it on your forearm: *Donors don't give because your organization is great. They give because **they** themselves are great.*

CHAPTER 8

I Have Bad News and Good News

Want to see a big squabble? Toss this question to a group of fundraisers: "**Do donors respond to need or to hope? Are they more likely to give when you tell the *bad news* about the problem you want to solve, or the *good news* about the impact they'll have?**"

Battle lines will form. On one side, the Bad News Army, battle-scarred and ready for a fight. Their argument goes like this:

> Donors want to solve problems. That's why we let them know *there is a problem* and they can help solve it.

Then there's the Good News Crew, their eyes bright and full of optimism. They counter the Bad News Army:

> Fundraising should be one place where you can *win*. We tell donors there's *hope*. That the problem will be solved.

If you were forced to join either the Bad News or the Good News group, you'd be better off with the former. In fundraising response tests, bad-news appeals almost always outpull hope-based good-news ones.

That's because happy-talk about how a charity has solved a problem fails to speak to the psychology of giving, which is a lot like the psychology of rescuing someone in trouble. If they've already been rescued, where's the urgency?

But there's a downside to Bad News fundraising. It can wear out donors over time. They keep being asked to solve problem after problem. They don't see progress. They can start to think giving doesn't really make a difference.

Bad News Fundraising yields short-term gain but long-term pain: you do well on any given campaign, but donor retention suffers, undermining future campaigns and slowly eroding your base of support.

I wish I could report that Good News Fundraising has the opposite effect: short-term pain but long-term gain. If that were true, it would be the better choice. Sadly, that's not so. Good News Fundraising gives you short-term pain *and* long-term pain. It gets lower response rates, and that automatically undermines donor retention. You lose today's *and* tomorrow's donations.

Bad News Fundraising might hurt you, but Good News Fundraising could kill you.

But you don't have to choose either Bad News or Good News fundraising. There's another way. In that squabble between the Bad News Army and the Good News Crew, there's a third group. It's much smaller, standing off to the side. They aren't fighting at all—just smiling knowingly.

I call them the *Balance Brigade*. They transcend the bad news and good news arguments. They're the ones who really do fundraising right. You can join them.

Here's how to do balanced fundraising

At first glance, balanced fundraising looks like Bad News Fundraising. It doesn't shy away from bad news. It focuses on the problem. The difference is that it also paints a picture of the better world donors can help create when they give. It's not afraid to say something like:

> The puppy huddles, shivering with cold and fear. His fur is matted, his tail between his legs, and he flinches every time you move—he thinks everything is going to be a beating.

Balanced fundraising pulls no punches. But it also uses language such as:

> You should see the transformation once you rescue them! Their fur is silky, they leap around, trying to kiss everyone—they're so happy to see their dog and human friends. And each one has that beautiful doggy smile that lets you know all is right with the world.

Balanced fundraising puts as much energy into describing the solution as the problem. Because a problem without a solution is cause for despair. And a solution without a problem is not only a logical fallacy, it's completely uninteresting. When you balance your fundraising message, you're telling your donors these truths:

> ▶ We share the pain and the triumph with you because we respect you. We know you can handle the pain, and we know you give because you look to the triumph you know can happen.
> ▶ The reason we're so insistent in describing the problem is we know it's something you care about.
> ▶ We're excited about the solution because with your help, it's in reach.

That's a platform for a successful fundraising message. It's also the foundation for a lasting relationship with donors.

Donors who are cultivated with balanced fundraising keep on giving, because giving feels the way giving ought to feel: like it *matters*.

If your fundraising is balanced, your donors will experience the double thrill of confronting real problems and being part of solutions. Giving to your organization will involve less guilt and more joy. Less like throwing money into a hole and more like a smart investment.

CHAPTER 9

Have a Clear Call
to Action

I live in one of those gentrified city neighborhoods that's full of fussy, hardworking professionals. You know the type of place: convenient location, nice housing, high prices, escarole salads.

It's a great place to live, and we stand ready to defend it against all threats.

Recently a locally owned and much-loved grocery store went up for sale. The proposed buyer was a national chain I'll call MegaMart. They planned to demolish our store and replace it with a monstrosity that would dwarf our cute houses and jam our streets with traffic from (gasp) other neighborhoods. Worse yet, it would no doubt fail to carry items like goat cheese, jicama root, and other ingredients critical to our lifestyle.

Neighbors swung into action to fight MegaMart. A committee formed. It produced yard signs that read:

Buy Locally.
Build Responsibly.
Build Community.

I'm not kidding. That was the official sign for neighbors who wanted to stop MegaMart. You might think a more effective sign would be something like:

No MegaMart!

After all, MegaMart was the issue at hand. But the committee felt it would be more effective to promote the philosophical underpinnings of the argument against large national chains in city neighborhoods in general. No mention of MegaMart. No call to action of any kind.

Big mistake.

Most people didn't have a clue what the signs were about. Even the sophisticated professionals of the neighborhood never quite grasped that *Buy Locally, Build Responsibly, Build Community* actually meant "No MegaMart."

Opposition has fizzled, and as of now it looks like we're going to get the MegaMart. At least they'll have low prices, guaranteed.

I don't know if we can blame our defeat on one ill-conceived yard sign. It was probably a symptom of a larger failure to communicate clearly.

Sadly, a similar thing happens often in fundraising.

We get so tied up in the philosophy of our cause that we think the philosophy *is* the cause. Then we forget to mention the cause.

Call to Action (often just CTA) is a bit of advertising industry lingo that every fundraiser should know and love. It means exactly what it says: it's the specific action you want people to take. Pick up the phone and dial a number. Go to the store and look for a specific product. Go to a website and sign up for something.

Or, in fundraising, make a gift to accomplish some specific good.

Maybe it sounds obvious, but when you don't call for action, you don't get action. Fundraisers jump through all kinds of hoops rather than make calls to action. Besides misguided appeals to philosophy like we made in my neighborhood, here are a few more ways we avoid calls to action:

Clever comparisons

Some fundraisers try to make their case with metaphors. They seem to think wordplay and visual puns are compelling.

The tragic earthquake and tsunami in Japan spawned a swarm of fundraising images that showed flags of Japan (red circle on white background) where the image was made to symbolize the disaster. In one, the red circle was cracked. In another, it was composed of squiggly lines like a seismograph makes during an earthquake.

The images looked good. But they didn't communicate a call to action.

The reason people give in times of disaster is because they're moved to compassion by the plight of fellow human beings. An abstract image symbolizing the disaster, no matter how clever, or how strong the design, fails to stir people to action. It doesn't touch the heart. It can't, because it isn't emotional.

In fundraising, you always do better by being completely *literal.* "Rush emergency supplies to people in the earthquake zone." Just tell and show what the problem and solution are. Leave the metaphors and symbolism to poets.

(If you hire an advertising agency to do your fundraising, there's a good chance they'll make this mistake.)

Journalism

Another way fundraisers avoid a call to action is to simply lay out the facts in an objective way. They carefully cover the who, what, where, when, and how.

Fundraisers who do this assume that if we simply tell donors what's going on, they'll know what action to take.

That's good journalism, but bad fundraising.

This approach is especially common when trying to raise money with email and social media. Time after time, a message points out that a problem exists. For donors to take action, they must make the leap from "There's a problem" to "I can do something about it."

It may be helpful to report on the terrible state of disrepair at Symphony Hall, but it's not fundraising until you specifically invite people to donate for repairs.

It may be blindingly obvious to you that the facts lead to the conclusion that one should give money. It's not obvious to everyone. Without a direct call to action, they'll go every which way—but mostly, they won't give.

Hinting around

Some fundraisers bury their call to action under layers of abstract verbal fluff. They say things like "Your support could bring hope to some special kids."

That's not straightforward enough to do the job. "Special kids" could apply to anyone on the planet who's under eighteen. "Hope" may be the thing with feathers that perches in the soul, but it has no single, specific meaning. Even the most direct word, "support," doesn't mean "donation" to everyone. Talk that way to donors, and they won't understand you.

A real call to action leaves nothing to the imagination. "Your gift of $25 or more—sent by December 31—will give low-income kids in our community soccer uniforms, so they can compete joyfully in this character-building sport."

Conversational warm-up

It's normal to start a conversation with easy, inconsequential small-talk ("Nice weather we're having"). We do this to gauge the mood of those we're talking to and to ease our way to the topic at hand, especially when the topic is difficult.

It's tempting to do this in fundraising, because asking for money is hard.

Resist! Time spent "warming up" to your asking is time for donors to lose interest.

Readers can't tell that your warm-up is, in fact, a warm-up, and that something more interesting is just around the corner. All they can tell is that you're being boring. They can easily find something more interesting to do than wait for you to get to the point.

It may feel strange to jump straight to the hard part of a conversation. In a face-to-face conversation you usually wouldn't do that. But in direct mail, email, print, or broadcast, if your message has warm-up time, donors won't stay with you.

*   *   *

I think the reason fundraisers use these ways of avoiding a call to action is because it feels, well, aggressive to come right out and ask for money.

Let me tell you a secret: Nobody is fooled by your fundraising appeal. They don't think they're getting a letter from a pal. They know you sent it to ask them for money. If you fail to ask, or pretend not to ask, all you accomplish is unclear communication.

So just ask.

Truth is, when you practice clear, call-to-action fundraising, you may get complaints from donors who feel you're too pushy. But here's what's strange: if you try indirect, no-call-to-action fundraising, *you'll also get complaints*, and for the very same reason—people think you're too pushy. Every fundraiser gets these complaints. The only sure-fire way to avoid them is never to raise money.

*   *   *

The final ingredient for a strong fundraising call to action is citing a *specific amount* of money that will accomplish specific activities:

- ▶ Give $1.79 to share a hot nutritious meal with a homeless person in the community.
- ▶ Save an entire acre of endangered rainforest with a gift of $12.
- ▶ Provide books for schools in poor neighborhoods for just $5 each.

Even in cases where it's tough to calculate a unit cost or where the costs are high (as with medical research), you should put the donor's giving in context:

- ▶ As we close in on a cure for this terrible disease, every gift—$25, $50, any amount that's right for you—brings the cure closer!

This dollar-specificity helps connect the donor to the cause in a practical way. It feels more real, because she can see what her giving does. It can also help overcome the common objection that her small gift won't make a difference.

When you get right down to it, successful fundraising is about giving donors the chance to take action. If you don't clearly specify that action, you stand little chance of succeeding.

CHAPTER 10

P.S. I Love You

Dear Friend,

I'm writing to you on a computer. That means I can easily revise until I'm satisfied with what I'm saying. And I can print out copies any time I want, because paper is cheap.

It wasn't always this way. People used to write letters by hand. Revising was a pain. Paper was a luxury. That's why some smart letter writer invented the P.S., an amazing paper- and labor-saving tool. It stands for *Post Scriptum*, Latin for "written after."

Think about it. All afternoon you've been laboriously scratching out a letter to Sir Herman. You're using a pen made from a feather, dipping it into the ink bottle every three or four words. It's a long letter because there's no phone, no email, no texting. Your hand is starting to ache, your neck is getting stiff, and you're running low on paper.

Finally, you get to the end of the letter and sign it. Then it hits you: "Heaven forfend! I forgot to ask Sir Herman to come in his best carriage when he visits fortnight next!"

Thank goodness you can put that in a P.S.

Of course things are different now. Even if we're sending a letter by post, we still write it with a word processor. If we think of something after we're finished, we can go back and insert it. Easy. No P.S. needed.

Unless you're raising money. That's right: every fundraising letter should have a P.S.

The fundraising P.S. has a very specific function. It's not like the one in your letter to Sir Herman, where you tacked on something you forgot to include earlier. It's a *re-statement of your main call to action*. One last time to say yet again what you want the reader to do:

P.S. Remember, it only costs $1.79 to share a complete Thanksgiving meal with a homeless person. Please send your gift by November 15 so we'll know how many we can feed this year.

P.S. The Museum's fiscal year ends September 30. Your gift by then will help keep our exhibits open for everyone.

P.S. In the time it took you to read this letter, three more people were diagnosed with Parkinson's disease. Please rush your gift to find new treatments—and the cure—for this disease.

Keep it simple and short. Just restate the call to action. Don't add any new ideas.

The P.S. is among the *first* parts of the message most donors read. They turn straight to the end of the letter, look at the signature, then their eyes drop down and take in the P.S.

Some then go back to the beginning of the letter and start reading. Others move right along and never bother to read the rest.

This behavior is well known in direct mail. And testing in email fundraising seems to show that people read their emails in a similar way. A P.S. in an email, as odd as that may seem, usually boosts response.

That means the P.S. might be the most-read part of your fundraising letter. For many of your readers, the P.S. is the *only* thing they'll see. Write it with that assumption in mind.

I hope every fundraising message you create is so well built it doesn't *need* a P.S. But please include one anyway.

Sincerely,

P.S. Don't omit the P.S.! It's a necessary part of an effective fundraising message.

PART III

The Design of Fundraising

Every three months, they do it again. The models stride down the catwalks, introducing the fashion industry's latest styles. Looking like creatures from another world.

The skirt looks like a nuclear cooling tower with thorns. There's a hat, or is it a paper plate? The shoes have been banned by the Geneva Convention. All in colors that make the model's skin look somewhat less healthy and glowing than Silly Putty.

Then the new styles show up in stores. To the relief of everyone, they're nothing like what the models wore. In fact, they're only slightly different from the clothes normal people have been wearing for years.

The designers may have weird ideas about what looks good, but they also know what normal men and women will buy. So they've learned to separate the designs that tickle their own fancies from the designs they sell. It's not a bad system.

I wish fundraising had something like that: a way for us to show off the designs we like—without uselessly foisting them on our donors. We could get it out of our systems and happily go back to the work that actually motivates people to give. That would save so much time and money!

Fundraising design that really works is typically old-fashioned, literal, "messy," and frustratingly utilitarian. It's all about getting people to respond, not being visually interesting or beautiful.

In the next few chapters we're going to look at real-life fundraising design—the kind that works. You may learn some principles you or your designer would rather not know, including:

► Type treatments that yield striking, modern design should almost never be used in fundraising.

► Fundraising depends on an almost manic use of underlining and other unattractive forms of emphasis.

► The images most everyone in your organization likes are often precisely the wrong images for fundraising.

► The three most important characteristics of fundraising design are: plain, corny, and obvious.

The next few chapters are *not* a primer on fundraising design. They won't make you a skillful designer. They simply offer a few key things to do and not do.

If you're a designer, it's possible this will frustrate you. But there's nothing I (or you) can do about it. If you want to raise funds, you have to play by donors' rules, not your own.

CHAPTER 11

Design for Older Eyes

They told me my voice was going to be squeaky and out of control for a while, but after that people would stop mistaking me for my mother on the phone. I was okay with that.

They told me that being a dad would turn me from an autonomous being into a full-time unpaid chauffeur. I was okay with that, too. (There are compensating factors.)

But nobody told me about bifocals. I'm not so okay with bifocals.

Turns out life is full of transitions, most of them inescapable. You'll always deal more successfully with people—adolescents and up—when you understand what they're going through.

Bifocals are inevitable once you reach a "certain age," which is somewhere around forty. Every pair of human eyes eventually develops presbyopia. I think that's Greek for "Your eyes don't work like they used to."

The older you are, the more severe your presbyopia. Above age sixty, virtually everyone has (or should have) bifocals. Which means . . . *your donors wear bifocals.*

If you don't have bifocals yet, let me tell you about them. They're okay most of the time. But reading is a challenge. You push the glasses up and down your nose. You crane your neck and tilt your head side to side, seeking the spot where the clarity is just right. You angle the paper to try and catch as much light as possible. Sometimes you just give up.

As a member of the presbyopic community, I have a proclamation:

> *Life is too short (as bifocals remind us) to spend a lot of time trying to read something that may or may not be of any value or interest.*

Design your fundraising to minimize the struggle. It doesn't matter how great a piece looks. If it's hard to read, it's downright rude. Remember, nobody is being forced to read your materials!

Of course any design that you hope will influence people must be clear, barrier free, and readable. That's true no matter who your audience is—even eagle-eyed youngsters who can see angels dancing on the head of a pin.

But the need for readability zooms to a top priority when you're communicating with older audiences. And that's usually the case with fundraising.

Some of what I'm about to say will displease some designers. They'll say design communicates emotions in intangible ways the written word can't. They'll point out that the way something looks and feels is its most fundamental level of communication. They'll say design sets the stage for copy, and that good design can have a donor halfway to yes before she's read a single word.

I completely agree. Good design does all that, and more.

But when design makes copy less readable while trying to accomplish its goals, it's just *bad design*. Please let that sink in. If it's hard to read, it's bad design. No matter how great it looks.

Here's the good news: great design and flawless readability aren't opposing values. Any designer who claims you sometimes have to sacrifice readability to get the right "look" doesn't know much about design. Such a designer is a ball and chain on your fundraising. No matter how stylish and tiny his glasses, he's not serving the cause.

Here, I'm going to focus on one area of design—type. There's a lot more to design than type, but it's the area where bad design most often emerges.

Here are some common type treatments that should never be part of your fundraising messages:

Sans-serif fonts

Sans-serif fonts (like Arial) are much harder to read than serif fonts like Minion, which you're reading now. In fact, studies have shown that sans-serif fonts steeply degrade readers' comprehension. They understand and remember less of what they read when it's set in a sans-serif font.

Many designers *love* sans-serif fonts because they're cleaner looking and more modern. Even most non-designers say they like sans-serif fonts better. So do focus groups.

But that stated preference means nothing when it comes to fundraising. We aren't trying to get people to admire our typography—we're trying to get them to vote with their wallets for our cause.

If your fundraising message is set in a serif font, more people will read, comprehend, and retain it. And that means they'll respond more. The tests are clear about this. Sans-serif fonts mean lost revenue. Think of these fonts the way Superman thinks of kryptonite.

There are two exceptions:

1. Headlines can be in sans-serif fonts and remain readable.

2. Online, sans-serif fonts are easier to read than serif fonts. In fact, you should avoid using serif fonts online as much as you avoid sans-serif fonts in print.

Type that's not black

Any color other than black for text is meaningfully harder to read.

Gray type is especially popular with designers, who will tell you that black type looks "harsh" or "dark." Whatever they might say about black text, it's really the only color you should be using.

You can get away with using other colors for headlines, where the negative impact of color is negligible. But even for headlines, make sure they're dark colors that contrast strongly against their backgrounds.

Type over a tint

Type over any color other than white is harder to read. The principle here is that maximum contrast between type and its background is the most readable. The further you stray from black type on a white background, the harder the copy is to read. If you must use a tinted background, keep it at 5 percent or less, and it'll still be readable.

Reverse type

Reverse type (white or light type over a dark background) is one of the worst readability-killers of all. It's even worse when it's over an image.

Unfortunately, reverse type is much loved by designers because it allows for striking designs. It may look great in a design portfolio, but it can crush fundraising revenue. That's a trade-off you might have a hard time defending.

If you put copy in reverse, assume it won't get read. Just don't do it!

Small type

Sometimes I wish 12-point type were the smallest possible font size. Because when you drop below 12, you start leaving readers behind.

Most newspapers and books are set at around 10-point, so in making 12-point a minimum, I'm asking you to do above-and-beyond design for readability. Remember the bifocals?

There are legitimate reasons for using smaller sizes in fundraising, the main one being for content that must be there but doesn't really have to be read. The stuff the lawyers and state regulators make you include.

But if you really hope donors will read something, don't make it smaller than 12-point. If you want to edge up above 12-point, better yet.

Designers will sometimes shrink the copy to make it fit in the space they have. That's usually the wrong solution to the problem. The right solution: edit the copy to make it fit at 12-point.

I remember reading about an experiment where college students were asked to wear shoes with weights, pants that made it hard to walk, and glasses that blurred their vision. The idea was to see if these young people's attitudes toward the elderly changed after they got a taste of what it's like to be old.

The kids were transformed. They saw the elderly as "real people." They were far more sympathetic. At least for a while.

All I can say about that is: *I want some of those vision-blurring glasses!* So I can give them to all fundraisers under the age of forty.

I think that would bring about some much-needed change in fundraising design.

CHAPTER 12

Don't Skimp on Emphasis

Sometimes we dream of a perfect, orderly life. No nasty shocks like cancelled flights or moody bosses. You never have a cold. No bad-hair days. Everything always works the way you want.

In that life, there are no surprises. Your car starts up every time you need it. Your keys are always right where you expect them to be. On the other hand, it's never Christmas or your birthday. You never see a sky-filling sunset that forces you to stop and stare. You don't unexpectedly run into an old friend.

Variety is what tells you where you are. And when. Even why. Life without it would be unbearable.

The written version of life without variation is a page of type without paragraph breaks, indents, or anything else to vary the flow of words. No matter how interesting the copy might be, it would be tough to read. Most readers would stop reading within seconds. Which, in fundraising, is the equivalent of sudden death.

That's why fundraising copy is so heavy on emphasis. Or, as critics of fundraising often put it, "All that tacky underlining."

A classic fundraising letter will often look like it came from an over-zealous college freshman with a blue pen and time on his hands.

If you think it's tacky, you're not alone. In fact, when people complain about fundraising, they often mention the underlining. It's ugly. Some even say it's rude.

I say *pshaw!* And I hope you will too.

If you don't underline, you'll get something a lot worse than grumbling about the way your materials look. You'll get *less response.*

The sad truth for writers is, most readers skim most of the time, stopping to read whatever grabs their attention. We're lucky if they do that much.

So we help them stop and read by grabbing their attention with underlining.

Every underline is a visual entry point into the letter, an invitation to pay more attention. Get their attention, and you've moved that much closer to a response.

Here's how to know what should be underlined. Look at a page (or screen) of copy and ask yourself, *What two or three phrases do I most want donors to read?* It might be one of these:

▶ **The call to action.**

   If you want to save our open beaches before the last stretch is walled off by condos, <u>send a gift now</u>!

▶ **An especially dramatic part of a story.**
We didn't realize how bad the famine was until we saw a group of children crawling along, <u>picking insects out of the dirt and eating them</u>.

▶ **Single words you'd say louder in speech.**
If you're the kind of person I think you are, you say <u>no</u> when you hear about dogs being forced to fight and kill each other.

Don't make underlines too long. Usually less than one line. If it goes two lines or more, the underline can defeat its own purpose and become visual noise.

Underlining isn't the only way to create emphasis and entry points in copy. Here are some others:

▶ Highlighting. A light yellow tint over a few words can really catch the eye.

▶ **Bold** or *italic* fonts. These shouldn't take the place of underlining, but they can be a good way to create secondary emphasis.

▶ Larger type. Yes, you can choose to increase the size of a phrase by a couple of points, and make it stand out.

▶ Sub-headlines. Do what many publications and websites do and break up copy with interesting headlines every now and them.

▶ Paragraphs with extra indentation. Just setting the left margin half an inch deeper for one paragraph will draw people's eyes.

▶ Handwritten notes in the margin. ← Like this!

These forms of emphasis are mainly geared for large blocks of text in print media, especially letters. But you can use them anywhere, including online.

The online medium has a special form of emphasis, the hyperlink. It isn't only an underline and a different color but it's an action readers can take. Include frequent hyperlinks in emails and on Web pages. Just make sure they link to places where you want readers to go—like a donation page—rather than away from the action.

Every page of copy should have at least one entry point. Two or three are better, but no more than four or five, depending on the size of the page. Too much emphasis is the same as no emphasis at all.

Whatever you do, don't forget the old fundraising writer's rhyme:

If I forget to underline,
My donor response will surely decline.

CHAPTER 13

Make Images
Work for You

It was Traffic Safety Week in the fourth grade, and I was thrilled. We got to draw safety posters, and I had the coolest topic ever up my sleeve.

You see, I'd just gotten a new winter jacket: navy blue, hooded, extra long, and—best of all—it had a reflective stripe around each upper arm. I could picture the cars, dazzled by the glow of my armbands, screeching to a halt blocks before they reached me. In my opinion, it was the snazziest, space-age, as-seen-on-TV safety feature on Earth. Just in time to show on my Traffic Safety Week poster.

The main fact you need to know about my poster is how well I drew. You've seen drawings made by chimpanzees? I would have been one of the better artists among the chimps.

For my Traffic Safety poster I drew myself wearing my nearly black, hooded coat, walking in the dark. There was a crescent moon in the upper right. If you looked really carefully, you might have noticed I'd drawn my coat's reflective arm-bands in white crayon, but they were lost in the jaggy disorderliness of the drawing. Below, I'd written: WEAR BRIGHT COLORS AFTER DARK!

I learned later that my teacher, Mrs. Blewitt, had called my parents, deeply concerned. Not about my lack of artistic ability, but about my attitude.

What she saw in my poster was a sloppy picture of a kid dressed entirely in black, creepily walking in the dark, in direct defiance of a standard safety message.

She thought it was sneering sarcasm, of the kind common among adolescents, but rare among fourth-graders. Being sarcastic about Traffic Safety was the equivalent of embracing Communism.

My parents set Mrs. Blewitt straight—my poster was earnest if incompetent. My bad-attitude phase was still a few years away.

But my poster didn't appear with the others in the Traffic Safety Week display. Mrs. Blewitt must have figured a well-meaning poster that even *looked* like it had a bad attitude posed a threat to the order and patriotism of the fourth grade.

It was my first experience of having my message undermined by a well-meant but inappropriate image. But not my last.

Imagery is a challenge in fundraising. The problem is seldom lack of skill, as it was for me in the fourth grade. Much more often it's because the images communicate the wrong information.

Most fundraisers agree that photos of people are a necessary part of successful fundraising messages. That's half right.

A great image can make all the difference. It can crystallize the message and drive home its emotional core more powerfully and memorably than words can.

If you've seen it, you'll never forget the famous photo of an emaciated child in southern Sudan, overcome with hunger, crouching face down on the ground; a few feet away hunches a vulture, staring at the child with hungry, evil eyes. That image helped unlock millions of donor dollars and probably resulted in countless lives saved. That's what the right photo can do.

But the wrong photo can deflate your message. It can undo the work of even the strongest copy.

There are three ways that photos most often go wrong in fundraising messages:

1. The photo contradicts the message

The words say, "Children are going hungry . . . won't you help them?" but there's a photo of happy, plump children. They don't look hungry. They don't look sad, worried, in pain, or even inconvenienced. The picture speaks more loudly than the words, and with more emotion. There might as well be a banner headline that says, "Don't Worry: The Kids Are Just Fine."

If you're telling donors that someone is suffering in poverty, use an image that shows someone suffering in poverty. They needn't be wailing their despair or covered with flies, but they shouldn't be grinning either.

2. The photo shows unsympathetic-looking people

The human face conveys a lot of information. A single expression, caught on film, can tell us more than several paragraphs of carefully written copy. Sometimes that expression discourages donors from giving.

Someone who appears to be glaring at the camera sends a hostile message. This happens often, because some people, when they're in pain or afraid, furrow their brow—it looks like they're scowling. That's not what they're doing, but that's how it looks. At a powerful, unconscious level, the message is "Go away. I don't like you." And that's just what donors will do. They'll go away. Who wants to reach out to someone who seems to be hostile toward you?

I've seen photos used in fundraising where subjects had what looked like a contemptuous sneer. Or a derisive grin. Or a furtive sidelong look. These images can drain all the compassion from a donor's heart and make her think that those in the picture are dishonest or undeserving.

Always study people's expressions in photos to make sure there's no unintended message waiting to chase donors away.

3. The photo is confusing

Sometimes your work doesn't look the same to you as it does to outsiders.

I once worked with a social service agency that helped homeless people get off the streets. For a brochure about their work, they chose a photo of one of their staff counseling some homeless men.

The photo looked like three guys lounging around in easy chairs.

To the organization's staff, it was an accurate depiction of their work. Counseling, after all, is talk, and it goes better when people are relaxed. But to most people, it looked like these guys were taking it easy, shooting the breeze, drinking beer.

Non-experts—that is, virtually everyone—expect charity to the homeless to look like some kind of active serving. Ladling soup, handing over blankets, doing medical checkups. When a photo fails to meet these expectations, it sends the wrong message, and it does so with more force than words.

Another common type of confusing photo is one that's meant to show that "we help a lot of people." A photo of a large group being helped usually looks like an unruly crowd, not an act of charity. Non-experts can't detect the good work that's happening. They see a mob.

These mistakes are common because they're hard for us to see. There's a kind of blindness that comes from too much knowledge. You know what the photo is about, so you can't clearly see what's on the surface. But the surface is the only thing most donors will see.

Here are two ways to overcome your blindness and choose winning images:

> ▶ Remove "I like" and "I dislike" from your photography criteria. Rely instead on what photos show and how they're

likely to affect others. How you respond isn't relevant. Worse, your response is likely to lead you astray.

As an insider to the cause, you feel rewarded by images of success. They validate your hard work. But to outsiders, images of success signal that there's no need for them to act. Images of unmet need are what motivate action. The most effective photos will probably not sit right with you. Seasoned fundraisers grow used to that fact.

► Enlist a non-expert to tell you what they see in the photo. They won't have the blinders of knowledge you have. Don't ask for a critique of its quality or correctness; just have them tell you what they see. Often, you'll be amazed by what you're missing.

I've told you the kinds of photos to avoid. Now here are some of the positive qualities to seek for a compelling fundraising image:

► Try to show direct eye contact with the subject. Eye contact is innately attention-grabbing, so it pulls viewers into the image. This is often the difference between a compelling photo that helps raise money and a dud that takes you nowhere.

► Use images of one person, rather than a group. It's far easier for a viewer to engage with one face than with a crowd.

► Photos of people usually work better than photos of objects. You may be asking donors to help you dig a well, but the well isn't the "product" you're selling. The product is the saved lives.

► Avoid stock photography. It lacks that sense of reality, and most people can detect the insincerity of it. It's better to use a lower quality of real people than a perfect but inauthentic stock photo.

If you know much about photography, you might be surprised and dismayed that I haven't said anything about technique: composition, tone, contrast—things professional photographers know how to manipulate.

That's because the reality shown in a photo is much more important than the technique. Of course, a technically good photo is better than a bad one. But fundraising isn't art. Excellence is measured by response, not technique.

And what if you don't have the right photo? *No image at all* is better than the wrong photo. Don't be afraid to let words do the work for you. That's far better than letting the wrong image hijack your message. This would have really paid off for me in the fourth grade!

CHAPTER 14

Plain, Corny, and Obvious

Sir Isaac Newton saw an apple fall from a tree. Instead of thinking about pie, like many of us might, he asked himself, *What caused the apple to rush toward the Earth like that?*

That led to his Law of Gravity. Which ultimately led to science as we know it.

But don't blame Newton for gravity. Before he came along, gravity made millions of apples fall from millions of trees for millions of years. Newton just paid more attention than others did.

A smart fundraising professional is a little like Sir Isaac Newton: a watcher. We watch our work drop into the postal system or the Internet. Most of it disappears forever, but some finds its way back to us with money. It mostly behaves in predictable ways. Sort of like gravity, though not quite as dependable.

In fact, through close observation, fundraisers have discovered three "Design Laws"—practices that, if we follow them well, encourage our fundraising messages to bear fruit. Those laws are:

1. Make it plain.
2. Make it corny.
3. Make it obvious.

Mind you, we didn't create these laws. We just observed that you get more response when you follow them. Let's look at each of the practices.

First Law: Make it plain

A piece of direct mail has to get noticed. If it gets noticed, it may get opened. If it gets opened, it may get read. If it gets read, it may get a response.

This fact leads many fundraisers to break the First Law: they over-design the envelope. Cover it with images and type. Sometimes artsy and beautiful, sometimes as busy as Times Square.

This is usually a mistake. (Not always; I'll get to that shortly.) In our over-marketed society, when someone's trying to get our attention everywhere we look, a whisper can have more impact than a shout.

In direct testing, an envelope with no image and no teaser outperforms one with a teaser about 75 percent of the time. A plain envelope is generally your best bet.

You might conclude, then, that teasers on envelopes are the equivalent of poison ivy, that it's just a bad idea to go near them.

I don't think so. It's just that most teasers are so bad they do more harm than good. You're better off with nothing. But an envelope with a *good* teaser always performs better than an unmarked envelope.

The main reason so many teasers fail to get their envelope opened is this: they leave no mystery. They give it away, leaving donors with no reason to open the envelope and look inside. Like these:

▶ Help us erase the shortfall and start our season in the black.

▶ Hungry children are waiting for you to say yes.

Why open an envelope that says that? You already know what's inside. Envelopes like that don't do very well.

Curiosity is a powerful motivator. Have you ever been to a nude beach? If you have, you know how unenticing it can be when everything is revealed.

I know of three main exceptions when being un-mysterious can be effective:

1. When you can make a straightforward, not-at-all mysterious statement that's top of mind and urgent for everyone. In the days after the 2011 earthquake and tsunami in Japan, *Japanese survivors are waiting for help* would have been an effective teaser.

2. When your fundraising call to action is a "good deal"— something that thrillingly stretches the generosity of the donor to do even more than usual. You can't go wrong with variations on *Matching funds will double your gift.*

3. In some cases, an envelope that has some variation of "Annual Fund Drive" works well. I'm amazed how well I've seen it do. It may seem boring—almost as if you're saying, "Here's your charity bill. Time to pay up"—but it taps into the expectations of many donors. It doesn't work for everyone, but it might be worth a try.

I've been talking about direct mail envelopes, because that's where the impact of plain design is most powerful. But "make it plain" is good advice almost everywhere in fundraising.

"Make it plain" also works online. In email, text-only messages are the equivalent of a plain envelope. They do better in testing nearly every time. (In fact, the only way I've found to beat a text-only email is when you have one of those rare and powerful images that do the talking for you.)

What's odd about the First Law is that *you should break it sometimes.*

If you use plain design most of the time, I've found you can get good results now and then with an "over-designed" envelope. Apparently, variety sometimes trumps the First Law.

Second Law: Make it corny

I've known fundraisers who've spent their whole careers point-lessly fighting the Second Law, trying to create classy, modern, nice-looking appeals they'd feel good about showing around. They might as well try to move Mt. Everest with a tooth-pick. Trying to beat the Second Law is a losing strategy and a sad waste of many hours and lakes of ink. Honestly, you're going to have to choose between a look that pleases you and a look that brings in revenue. Or you can learn to enjoy corny design. (That's not so hard, given that the corny stuff raises more money.)

Corny design that works well in fundraising has these features:

▶ **Old-fashioned.** Dated. Think about it: most donors are older. Their idea of good-looking design was formed decades before yours and mine. It doesn't look old-fashioned to them; it looks normal.

▶ **Unsophisticated.** Elegant, art-school design may be what you'd rather look at—I know I would—but it's not going to help you raise money. If it's Thanksgiving, you can hardly go wrong with a silly turkey or a smiling pilgrim wearing a hat with a buckle. It's not classy, not high-end, but it works. Unsubtle symbols, loud colors, blocky layout—they all do well in fundraising.

▶ **Ugly.** When it seems rough, unprofessional, even clunky, you're usually on the right track. I don't mean ugly as in hard to read, impossible to navigate, or communicating the wrong message. That's not ugly design; it's just *bad design*. But if a design makes you cringe, if you think your friends would make fun of you for using it—there's a good chance it's going to do well in fundraising. (Personally, I hesitate to call design that makes the world a better place "ugly"—that seems more like a definition of "beautiful.")

I can't count how many times I've wondered if we'd made the design of a fundraising message *too corny*. So old-fashioned, unsophisticated, and ugly that it was going to turn off donors and do poorly. Like tacky little clip-art Christmas decorations that would turn the stomach of any self-respecting art student.

So far, that has never happened. Corny works. It doesn't seem to be possible to be *too corny*.

I said earlier that you can disobey the First Law now and then. Don't try to break Second Law. You'll regret it.

Third Law: Make it obvious

I like puzzles. Give me a few idle moments and a crossword or a Sudoku, and I'm happy. Like most people, I like the small victories of discovering something that's hidden.

But I view with perfect hatred any puzzle I'm *forced* to do. Complicated tax forms. Expense reports that won't reconcile. Anything to do with insurance.

You aren't the IRS. Donors can walk away from your puzzle the moment they realize they're having to work to figure out what you're saying.

Don't let that happen! Design everything so it's completely puzzle free:

▸ Place a dotted line over every perforation or anyplace you want people to cut or tear. If there's no perforation, add a little graphic of scissors cutting along the line to really make it clear.

▸ Put important points in bigger and bolder type.

▸ Have arrows pointing at places where you want people to look.

▸ Include a phrase like "Please turn page" at the bottom of the page when copy continues on to the other side.

▸ Use plenty of underlining.

▸ Use starbursts to call attention to key points.

The main thing to remember about making it obvious is this: if the donor has to figure it out, she probably won't. And hardly anything is self-evident.

*   *   *

Plain. Corny. Obvious. These Three Laws will cause some designers and others who prefer a high-end look to grind their teeth with annoyance. I've known some who walked away from fundraising because they couldn't stand working that way. That's a wise choice, and I'd advise it to any designer who can't live with the reality of what works in fundraising.

But those who grasp it can grow to love it. Plain, corny, and obvious design can have the world-changing beauty of an apple gently dropping to earth while a thinker watches and wonders.

PART IV

The Mental Game of Fundraising

I f you go to the symphony, you've seen the bass players: they're the guys in the back with the big standing string instruments.

They may look calm and aloof from where you're sitting, but they're sweating bullets. I know. I'm a bass player.

The problem is, the bass is hard to play in tune. I'm not looking for sympathy, but *hard* isn't quite the right word for it; *herculean* captures it a little better.

The strings run along a thirty-six-inch fingerboard. To get the right note, you must hold down a string at precisely the right place. If you miss that spot, by even a razor-thin margin, you're out of tune. You're the cause of sourness and disorder that momentarily infects the entire orchestra.

As a bass player, you put many years and vast energy into learning where to place your fingers. You train every muscle, nerve, and tendon from your shoulder blades to your fingertips to hit that tiny, moving target again and again. To find it by feel and muscle memory.

But that doesn't really work. You improve over time, but you can never count on fingering the right note until you learn this secret: no matter how well you train yourself, you can't play in tune unless you *hear each note first.*

The in-tune note must sound inside your mind. When it does, it guides your finger more accurately than all your hours of physical training.

There's a mental component to most activities. Athletes know this. You can watch them see ahead to the play they're about to make. Even my cat, who's no feline Rhodes Scholar, knows it. Before she leaps from the couch to the chair across the room, she moves her head up and down, as if tracing her own arc through the air.

So it's no surprise that there's a mental component to fundraising.

You can learn the techniques, memorize the facts, and master all the details a fundraiser needs to know—but if you don't have the right mental game, you'll miss the target more often than not. You'll make wrong assumptions about what donors want to support. You'll misconstrue what donors are telling you. You might even make the terrible error of thinking fundraising is a shameful activity.

In these final chapters, we'll explore the mental game of fundraising. I'll show you some ways to think about the work we do and translate thought into action. We'll look into:

▶ The one thing you should *never* do in fundraising that most people do all the time.

▶ Some key facts about most donors that fundraisers often ignore.

▶ Some beliefs about fundraising that aren't true, though almost everyone believes them.

▶ Most important, the truth about what's really going on when we encourage people to financially support our causes. (It's good news. Very, very good news.)

When you internalize all of this, you'll find fundraising to be a different sort of activity. More joyful, less frustrating. You'll think more clearly and act more boldly. You'll develop better instincts for innovation. You'll more confidently navigate hard times and unexpected challenges. You'll find you can adjust to the shifting demographic, cultural, and technological worlds we operate in.

You'll be a lot more in tune. And that not only means more success—it's more fun, too.

Self-Centric Fundraising

You know the story of the Boy Who Cried Wolf. You probably haven't heard about his brother, who replaced him in the pasture shortly after his untimely demise.

Within minutes of arriving at the pasture, the new boy saw a wolf—word had gone around the wolf community that the sheep outside that particular village made an easy meal. The wolf was stalking back and forth at the edge of the pasture, a greenish cast to his eyes.

The boy cupped his hands around his mouth and cried, "Wo"—and then stopped himself.

"I can't cry 'wolf,'" he thought. "That's what my brother did. I've got to distinguish myself. I'm more educated and creative than he was."

One eye on the approaching wolf, he sat and thought until he remembered the scientific name for the wolf: *canis lupus*.

"Now that's *good*," the boy said. "That's *me*. I'd come running if I heard that. It'll remind everyone that I went to school, that I read a lot, that I'm an intellectual who chooses his words carefully. I'll cry 'canis lupus' and enhance my personal brand."

So he stood up and cried, "Canis lupus! Canis lupus!" He tried to use a calm and dignified tone, because that felt more appropriate than hoarse bellowing.

The few villagers who heard him shook their heads and smiled. "Crazy kid," they said. "At least he isn't a troublemaker like his brother." They had no idea what he was crying about.

So the wolf pounced on the nearest sheep and ate it. Then a dozen other wolves swarmed out of the forest. They ate all the sheep. Then they ate the boy, too. And, contrary to what you may have read in other tales, once a wolf eats you, your part in the story is over.

Almost every fundraiser I know is afraid of being perceived as a Boy Who Cried Wolf—afraid their fundraising will lose its ring of truth and be heard as a false alarm.

It would be more realistic to fear being the Boy Who Cried Canis Lupus. Because being misunderstood happens to fundraisers far more often than being disbelieved. Too many messages fail to reach donors because fundraisers cater to their own tastes—and end up making no sense to their donors.

It's one of the most common errors we make: *Self-Centric Fundraising*.

Self-Centric Fundraising starts with this assumption: *if it moves me, it's moving*. You carefully craft the message you think you would respond to.

That's the mistake.

You are not your donors. You're almost certainly younger. You're probably more educated, especially about marketing. Things don't look the same to you as they do to them.

But your level of attention is what really separates you from your donors. You pay close attention to every word of your fundraising. (I hope you do, anyway.) You ponder the nuance of every phrase. This focus magnifies everything for you. It can cause clarity to seem like over-simplification. It can make emotion seem like a ridiculous sob story.

Furthermore, you see *everything* you produce. That can give you the sensation that your messages are numbingly repetitive. Your donors, though, only see a fraction of what you do.

Most fundraisers want to make their messages more complex and intellectual than donors are likely to understand. They want their words to be less emotional than what it takes to touch donors' hearts. They also tend to vary their messaging so often that donors have trouble getting a handle on what the central message really is.

Fundraisers make these choices because that's what feels right to them.

But that's not all. There's a bigger danger, the wolf in the pasture, so to speak. Self-Centric Fundraising is a big mistake because *everyone's conscious opinions about fundraising are automatically wrong.*

Always. No exceptions. Your conscious opinions are wrong. Your spouse's opinions are wrong. So are your consultants'.

Even your donors' conscious opinions about the quality of your fundraising are completely and irredeemably wrong.

That's because consciously judging a fundraising message for its quality is nothing at all like encountering it in real life. The judging mind is tainted with what it prefers and believes. And the judging mind has no clue what the non-judging mind actually wants.

In real life—when you aren't judging, but living—you don't think about an abstract notion like quality. The message either gets your attention, stirs your heart, and moves you to action . . . or it doesn't.

Donor focus groups show how far people's judgments are from real life. If you show a focus group an assortment of direct mail and ask them to react—*everyone hates the stuff that works best*. They say they'd *never* respond to the very pieces that are getting the most response from people just like them.

And the example they love, fawn all over, and swear they'd respond to? Try it in the mail, and it will crater like a meteor on the dark side of the moon.

They aren't lying. They're giving an honest accounting of their conscious opinions.

It's simply impossible to stand outside yourself and tell an accurate story about how you would respond. Nobody can do it.

The stuff you think is good, that makes you feel proud and happy . . . if it showed up in your mailbox out of the blue, the way real fundraising does, *you wouldn't respond to it.* The stuff you love tickles a certain part of your conscious brain. It's just not the same part that prompts you to give.

The best fundraisers know this odd truth: *I love this* really means *people aren't going to respond to this.* Most fundraising consultants know a related truth: *if my client loves it, it's not going to do very well.*

Here are some of the destructive things that happen when you employ Self-Centric Fundraising:

You lose the emotion

If you have an emotional connection with your cause (and I hope you do), you forged that connection some time ago. You experienced something that brought you to your feet, ready to devote a serious chunk of your life to the cause. Now the honeymoon is over. You've settled in to make the relationship stable and prosperous.

There's nothing wrong with that. But never forget that where you are today is different from where you started out. Your connection back then was shallow, and you were relatively ignorant. Most of your donors are like you were back then, probably even more so.

What persuades you now in your post-emotional, make-it-work phase isn't even close to what reaches donors. Your reasons for caring are smart, well-formed, and sophisticated. But too flat, rational, and antiseptic to move donors.

Consider hunger, a cause that raises billions of dollars every year.

To be exact, hunger is a feeling you get in your stomach when it's time to eat. We all feel hunger, almost every day.

Less precisely, hunger also means the inability of people to get the food they need—because of poverty, famine, war, or disaster. Hunger in that sense has almost nothing to do with the hunger you and I know.

Global hunger is a big and complex problem. With big and complex solutions. You can't grab a sandwich and make it go away. Not even a billion sandwiches would make it go away.

Experts who work on hunger prefer to call it "food insecurity." It's a more accurate term.

The problem is, most donors don't know what food insecurity is. Even when they do, the term has no emotional punch, and no connection to anything they know.

If your cause is fighting hunger and you engage in Self-Centric Fundraising, you may want to talk about food insecurity. You'll be pleased by how precise your message is. And your donors will sit on their hands, waiting to hear about something that moves them. Like hunger.

You don't focus on donors

You're proud of your work and your organization. You should be. Your organization's excellence, its methodology, and its history are the reasons you're involved.

Those facts aren't compelling for donors. Remember this: donors don't give because of what *you* are; they give because of who *they* are.

Here's a passage I'd characterize as donor-focused fundraising:

You're someone who has a heart for little children. You want to see them live a happy and full life and grow up into healthy, happy adults.

To an insider, that passage is painfully irrelevant. It's not about the real issue or the real solutions. And it's embarrassingly sentimental.

With Self-Centric Fundraising, you'd replace that passage with a stream of slam-dunk facts that prove why a gift to your organization is effective, efficient, and smart. Like this:

In the next fiscal year, we are going to implement an innovative civil society project that will spur economic activity and lead eventually to an astounding 62 percent reduction in child/infant mortality.

All very correct, true—and beside the point. You'd get yawns, not gifts.

If you want gifts, you must frame your case as the donor's opportunity to change the world.

Those important facts about your organization? Some of them belong in your message. But they play second fiddle to the donors' motivations for giving.

Your copy reads like inter-office memos

I once had a client say about a piece I'd written, "This sounds like a letter to my mother." I was about to respond, "What a nice compliment," when I saw the look on her face. She hated that letter-to-mother quality. It wasn't professional.

The working world demands a level of decorum. We comport ourselves as even-tempered professionals. Our documents are clean, clear, and straightforward. We get good at that. We value it.

But fundraising doesn't live in the cubicles and carpeted offices of the business world.

Fundraising belongs to a messier, more passionate world that includes love letters, ransom notes, pleas for mercy, and outbreaks of religious fervor. The standards of business communication are just roadblocks in that world.

If you drag your fundraising into the world of professional communications, you'll leave donors cold and untouched.

A businesslike passage about a children's cancer center might sound like this:

Please consider supporting the 124 children (aged one to seventeen) in our hospital. A third of them are receiving advanced chemotherapy. Many of the rest are taking part in Phase I or Phase II clinical trials of new and promising therapies that could save the lives of future patients.

The non-businesslike successful fundraising approach would go more like this:

Six-year-old Chelsea hugged her teddy bear tight. "Teddy's hair didn't fall out," she said, patting her own bald head. "So he's my good-luck bear. He's going to help me get better from cancer." Teddy may be Chelsea's good-luck bear, but you can have a part in her fight against cancer by sending a gift today.

Many meaningful and important facts are omitted from the second version. That's because those facts aren't what motivate donors to give.

*   *   *

There's a reason Self-Centric Fundraising is so common: Donor-Centric Fundraising is a lot harder to do.

So let me tell you a secret—*the* secret—that allows fundraisers to escape Self-Centric Fundraising:

Look at what has motivated donors before. Pay close attention to the messages that have worked for you in the past. If they're in short supply, find out what works for other organizations.

Turn off that evaluating voice that tells you what you like. Lean instead on knowledge about who your donors are, what they respond to.

Ban from your vocabulary comments like:

► I like that.
► I hate that.
► I'd respond to that.
► I'd be ashamed to show this to my friends.

Almost any judgment with *I* in it will move you in the wrong direction. It doesn't throw light on the most important question: will donors respond?

Instead, ask questions like these:

> ► Is it emotional? Is it aimed at the heart, or is it a recitation of facts?
> ► Is it clear, easy to understand, even for someone with no knowledge about the subject?
> ► Is it simple? Can the essence of the message be made clear and compelling in one sentence?

It's hard to do fundraising right. It takes discipline and focus to put aside your own preferences. Self-Centric Fundraising is a feel-good path. It gives you the temporary illusion of excellence, because you like what you see. But, like the Boy Who Cried Canis Lupus, you won't feel good for very long.

CHAPTER 16

Three Things You Should Know About Donors

Y ou can learn a lot from the cardboard signs of street
fundraisers. Like this one I saw recently in Seattle:

> Wounded vet
> Can't work
> Please help
> God bless!

Not bad. It showed the need. It answered a common objection: "Why don't you get a job?" It was polite, patriotic, and slightly religious. And it had a direct ask. What more could he need?

Problem was, nobody was giving the guy a penny.

The next fellow, not thirty feet down the block, was getting all the donations. People were stopping, chatting with him— and filling his bucket with bills. His sign said:

> My father was killed by ninjas
> Need money for karate lessons

Come on! He was raking in the funds with a self-evident lie! Just a goofy story and a little smirk.

Why was the second sign pulling in the money?

Location! We were on Pike Street. It connects downtown Seattle with Capitol Hill, home to many young, hip, aspiring artists/poets/musicians who make up the Seattle "scene."

Most people passing the two signs were jaded, irony-loving hipsters. The earnest appeal of a struggling wounded veteran wasn't interesting to them. It didn't cut through the clutter of the city landscape. The quirky, made-up story of the other guy got their attention and delighted them. So they gave.

Knowing your audience makes all the difference.

The first fellow did everything right but didn't know his Pike Street audience. So all his fundraising technique went to waste.

Don't let that happen to you!

I don't know your audience, but I do know some demographic facts about donors in general. Knowing these and letting them shape your fundraising will give you an advantage like that enjoyed by the karate-lessons guy.

Donors are more likely to be women

Women outnumber men on most donor lists by about two to one. That's mainly because the male and female minds are different.

In general, women are more empathetic and more relationship minded than men. (These are tendencies, not absolutes. We all know women who are as empathetic as bricks, and men who can out-relationship Dear Abby.)

To put the difference in fundraising terms: women prefer to improve relationships; men prefer to fix problems.

Suppose you need to raise funds to dig wells in impoverished communities:

▶ If you wanted to persuade women to give, you'd describe how those who need the wells *feel*: their pain, their sadness, their lack of hope. You'd show how it affected families—mothers who lost their children, fathers not able to provide. You'd present the solution you're asking the donor to provide in terms of the joy, relief, and healing it would bring.

▶ If on the other hand you wanted to reach men, you'd frame the problem as a broken system. You'd describe the ways it causes people to suffer: the illnesses, the deaths, the inability to become self-sufficient. Your solution would be the "repair" that's needed, and you'd describe how much better everything would function after the donor gave.

Of course, most organizations, most of the time, are talking to both men and women. The best fundraising blends elements of both approaches.

In my experience, many fundraisers—including women—ignore women donors. They consistently make almost purely "masculine" cases for support, making it about fixing things rather than about relationships. That's a missed opportunity and a serious error.

Unless you specifically know otherwise, assume your audience is a lot more women than men. Don't overlook the majority of your donors.

Donors are more likely to be older

Most nonprofits have average donor ages well above sixty-five. This demographic is more pronounced than the tilt toward women. Donors under age fifty are rare, and typically they have extremely low retention rates. Even if you manage to snag young donors, you're going to be hard-pressed to keep them.

Ground-breaking research in the last few years has given us insight into how the human brain works,[*] including how it changes with age. Changes in brain chemistry cause older people to be more empathetic and emotional. Combine these tendencies with the wisdom and perspective that often come

---

[*] For a lot more practical applications of this new research, read *Brainfluence: 100 Ways to Persuade and Convince Consumers with Neuromarketing*, by Roger Dooley.

from age, and you see why older people are more predisposed to charitable giving. They typically have:

- ▶ An enhanced sense of connectedness with others and responsibility for the world around them.
- ▶ A sense that their chance to make a difference is running short.
- ▶ A need to "give back" for the blessings they've received in life.
- ▶ A desire to reconnect with their faith (more on that, and what it means for fundraising, shortly).
- ▶ Less interest in buying stuff, like fashionable clothes or the latest gadgets.
- ▶ More income and time as a result of children leaving home.

All of which helps to explain why almost all donor files are dominated by older people.

As we've already discussed with bifocals, design must take into account our donors' ages. But we also need to adjust the language we use and the ways we persuade. For example:

- ▶ Avoid slang and jargon. Older readers are less likely to understand and more likely to interpret it negatively. The word "lame" may clearly mean "low quality" to you or me; to many older people, it means an injured leg. And a word like "sustainable"—perfectly useful and very popular among nonprofits—has little meaning to your donors.

▶ Don't rely on novelty. For young people, the very fact that something is new, cutting-edge, or innovative is a high recommendation. Older people are less likely to be impressed with newness. Some are even suspicious of it.

▶ Use hype sparingly. Calling something "great," "incredible," or the "best ever" (or the "worst") tends to fall flat with older audiences. They don't believe it. They weren't born yesterday! In fact, go light on adjectives and adverbs in general. They add little value to your argument.

▶ Emphasize a "good deal." Older people are more cost conscious. It pays to stress value: The low cost of providing a meal or other help. Matching funds that will multiply the value of a gift. Other forms of leverage that make your offer appeal to value seekers.

▶ Finally, don't over-rely on technology. Older people adopt new technology later than others. That means exciting new developments like social media platforms, QR codes, smartphone apps, and other new-fangled technologies aren't likely to have much impact with today's donors.

That said, older people *are* taking to the Internet in a big way, which is why email fundraising is growing so fast.

Donors are much more likely to be religious

The connection between religious practice and charitable giving is overwhelming. Across the board, religious people are the backbone of philanthropy—not only to religious organizations and houses of worship but to all types of causes. Most likely, a large percentage of your donors are people of faith.

Virtually all faiths encourage (or even command) charitable giving. It's an integral part of spiritual practice and is typically taught to children. It's a habit that strengthens through the years, and few non-religious people match it.

If you're in a religious organization, you know what to do with this information: talk to your donors in the faith language you share with them.

If your organization isn't religious, your operating principle should be something like the Hippocratic Oath: *do no harm.*

► **Respect donors' faith.** If you and most of your friends consider religious people to be superstitious or uninformed, it's easy to let drop a thoughtless barb. Learn to filter these thoughts in all your dealings with donors.

► **Don't be afraid of their world.** Most people of faith live in a highly spiritual world. They see the work of God all around them, and tend to see most good things, including your organization's work, as "blessings" from above. Non-specific, semi-religious terms (like *blessings*) can make donors feel at home.

► **Be aware of the diversity of religion.** There's a wide variety of religious practice and culture among Christian groups. There's also a fast-growing population of non-Christian believers throughout the West. Religious people are far from monolithic. (I once read a fundraising appeal in which the signer talked about attending "mass" in a rural Baptist chapel. She might as well have headlined her message, "I don't have a clue!")

▶ **Don't pretend to be something you're not.** If your organization doesn't follow a faith tradition, don't try to curry favor with those who do by "faking it." If you don't normally talk about Jesus (or Mohammed or Buddha), don't try. You'll get it wrong. Religious donors are used to and comfortable with giving to non-religious causes. They're okay with you as you are! And if you are in a religious organization, don't hide your light under a bushel.

*   *   *

It's possible your donors aren't typical. Your cause, your history, or the media you use to attract donors could skew your donor file away from the female/elderly/religious norm.

Possible, but not likely.

The responsible approach is to assume a female-skewed, older, and religious group of donors unless you have proof otherwise.

Oh, and there's one other fact about donors that you really need to know:

Donors donate.

They give because they want to. They aren't being annoyed or cajoled into giving against their will.

They want to change the world.

They want a connection with your cause.

They know giving feels good.

Some fundraisers forget this and approach their donors as if asking is an imposition. It isn't. Fundraising is a *welcome* part of most donors' lives.

As you tune in to who your donors really are, you'll begin seeing consistently strong results from your fundraising. Just like the guy on Pike Street whose dad was knocked off by ninjas.

CHAPTER 17

Three Deadly Fundraising Myths

I n the high orchard country of the Pacific Northwest, there are a critical few weeks each spring when the buds emerge on the fruit trees. If the buds freeze, it can cause deformed fruit. Or no fruit at all. Frost—which happens every year—can devastate a crop and ruin a grower's livelihood.

A long time ago, the growers discovered a way to stave off freezing: smudge pots. These are ovens or barrels that produce thick, black smoke. A lot of it. They sit among the trees and burn old crankcase oil, tarpaper, tires—anything that burns dirty. The smoke insulated the buds from the cold, or so the growers thought.

On spring nights that threatened frost, the growers lit their smudge pots. The valleys would fill with creeping, noxious smoke. It gave everyone hacking coughs and all kinds of breathing problems.

The daily plague of smudge-pot smoke made orchard country a nasty place to live in early spring. Everyone hated it, but what could they do? If a fruit crop failed, they'd all suffer.

And apparently, the smudge pots worked. Orchards that used them had less frost damage.

We now know the smoke had nothing to do with it. The burning created turbulence that mixed layers of cold and warm air. That kept the temperature just above freezing. Clean-burning smudge pots would have done just as well. Or, better yet, huge fans. That's what you'll mostly see in the orchards these days, thank goodness.

The need for smoke was a myth. It came from reasonable—but wrong—interpretations of what the growers observed: more smoke, less frost damage. Year after year, they pointlessly filled their communities with choking smoke. As long as they believed the smoke was what saved the fruit, they really had no other choice.

Fundraising is plagued with smudge-pot myths: mistaken beliefs that lead us to destructive practices.

Here are three of the most common. Each one is false. Each one produces clouds of nasty smoke you don't have to put up with.

The myth of Too Much Mail

The specter of Too Much Mail haunts the dreams of many fundraisers. After all, it's the thing donors most often complain about. And we do send an awful lot of mail, don't we?

It's easy to conclude there's simmering anger that's about to boil over into a wide-scale donor revolt. They'll get fed up with all that mail and storm out on us en masse.

Good news: there's no evidence that this has ever happened or is likely to happen. In fact, all the evidence I've seen (and I've seen a lot) shows that more donor contact means more revenue, both in the short and long terms. Further, cutting back on donor contact almost always leads not only to less revenue but also to weaker donor retention.

In other words, *you're in a lot more danger from sending too little mail than from sending too much.*

So why are donors complaining?

There's no question they get an impressive volume of mail every day—from charities, catalogs, credit cards, gutter cleaners. It all adds up to a packed-full mailbox, day after day, much of the contents unwanted.

But most of it is *not* from you.

Think about it: a typical donor gets at least 10 pieces of unsolicited mail every delivery day. That's 3,000 pieces a year.

If you write to a donor twelve times a year, you're sending 0.4 percent of her yearly total. If you stopped mailing, the daily average would drop from 10 to 9.96. Not a meaningful difference for your donor.

But for you, that cutback would mean lost revenue, forever. A loss of hundreds, maybe thousands, of dollars from each donor.

You'll never solve the Too-Much-Mail problem if you treat it as a numbers game. The real issue is the relevance of the mail, not the volume.

What sets off many of the complaints is a box-full of junk that doesn't make sense. *Who thinks I need more credit cards with high interest rates? Who's guessing I want faux Native American themed clothing? Who got the idea I want to elect Republicans to the House of Representatives? Why do I get all this dumb, wasteful, annoying junk mail?*

You escape that diatribe if your material doesn't trigger the *why*. When your mail is relevant, people *know* why you sent it.

Relevant mail is welcome. It fits into the donor's world. It's about her. It talks about issues she's concerned with. It's relational, real, and it makes her feel empowered and connected.

When your fundraising is like that, you'll get fewer complaints—even if you send a lot of mail. I've worked with organizations that sent more than thirty fundraising pieces a year—and they got fewer complaints than some that sent twelve. The difference? Relevance.

The surest way to chase away your donors is to make all your messages about *you*, not the donor. Even one or two messages like that can feel like a deluge of junk mail. That's how you slip into irrelevance. You aren't likely to get a lot of complaints about it. But donors will silently fade away without saying anything.

The myth of the Rested Donor

The myth goes like this: once a donor gives, you should let him "rest" from hearing from you. This allows him to rejuvenate from the rigors of giving. If you ask too soon, before he's fully recovered, you'll do irreparable damage.

I've never seen evidence to support this. I haven't even heard a plausible hypothesis for why it might be true.

They say *Absence makes the heart grow fonder.* They're largely wrong about that. Can you think of any healthy human relationship that improves with no communication? Donors who don't hear from an organization for months after they've given are far less likely to ever give again.

Here's the fact: *the more recently a donor gave, the more likely he is to give again.*

Stop for a moment and take that in. It's one of the most important and useful truths in fundraising. *The more recently a donor gave, the more likely he is to give again.*

While you're letting your donor "rest," every other charity she gives to, and many more who are renting her name, are in her mailbox, giving her reasons to donate. During that "warm glow" period—that good feeling that came from giving to you—you're the only one absent.

With every passing week, the chance that you'll fade from the donor's memory grows. If you give a donor enough "rest," you can count on losing her forever.

The myth of the Killer Complaints

If you say anything at all to a large group of people, some of them will complain. That's a fact of life.

Politicians know it. So do TV producers and anyone else in media. Even the artists who create comic strips are intimate with complaints.

Fundraising is no different. Some donors complain no matter what you do. They complain about the amount of mail they get (see the myth of Too Much Mail, above). They complain that mailings are too expensive. Or too cheap. They complain about your sense of urgency, your grammar, your color choices. They complain that you sent—or didn't send—address labels. I once got an angry letter from a donor because a photo in my newsletter showed a Third World child in an emergency feeding program holding his spoon wrong. (Apparently, we were failing to teach the children proper values.)

It feels bad when donors complain. But about all that gets hurt by complaints is your feelings. Still, I've seen nonprofits so fearful of donor complaints that they scrapped successful campaigns. All because of a couple dozen complainers.

It seems any disgruntled person with the energy to write a note or an email has more power than the thousands of satisfied donors who voted "yes" *with their wallets* for your cause.

All fundraising programs generate complaints. In fact, the more successful the program, the more complaints. That's the nature of motivation. When you make a strong case for a gift, you put real emotions in play. Urgency and need—keys to successful fundraising—can make people feel uncomfortable. And some uncomfortable people complain.

That's not to say you should ignore complainers. Pay close attention to them. After all, they care enough to communicate with you. They're giving you a chance to serve them better and turn negative feelings into positive experiences. If you handle it well, you can turn a complainer into a more loyal friend than ever.

You may need to make changes for a complainer. If she says you send her too much mail, send her less. But never change your entire fundraising program to satisfy one or ten or even a hundred complainers. Only program-wide results should guide how you act program wide.

*   *   *

What these three myths have in common is a deadly belief that *fundraising hurts donors.*

I've heard expressed like this: "It's like we're giving our donors an electric shock every six weeks!"

Ouch!

If you think your fundraising is a painful experience for your donors, you're probably right. That's because you aren't approaching it as a relationship. You're just holding your nose and sending out another terrible appeal as often as you can stomach it.

Don't do that! Treat your fundraising as a relationship—a reciprocal, give-and-take between your cause and the good people who make it possible.

That way you have a chance of getting it right. Your messages will reflect the relational approach.

You'll treat donors with respect. You'll be thankful for their giving. You'll tell them they make a difference. You'll ask on *their* terms. And your asking will be as welcome as your thanking.

That's how fundraising can be.

But first, put away those smudge-pot myths. They're filling the valley of fundraising with nasty, choking smoke—and they aren't doing anything useful.

CHAPTER 18

Proud to Be a Fundraiser

"You stepped on my violin," she said, the moment I entered the room. "You smashed it. It can't be fixed." Her eyes were wide with an expression somewhere between fear and anger.

"Hi, Mom," I said.

Visiting her was like this now. Bedridden, in a nursing home, she was in her final months of a long battle with Parkinson's disease. Paranoid delusions were devouring more and more of her mind.

If I didn't respond to her accusations, she'd usually move along to other topics. Not this time. Delusions about the destruction of her violin were especially painful for her. She wasn't ready to change the subject.

"That violin is irreplaceable," she said. "Why did you do it?"

"Your violin is fine," I said, unwisely entering the premise of the delusion. "We're keeping it safe." The shape of her skull was clearly visible: the sharp corner at the back of her jaw, the depressions at her temples, the wide sockets around her eyes.

As she sometimes did when she grew frustrated with me, she began to scream: a piercing, high monotone with a harsh edge, as if it were being ripped from her throat. But because she was so weak, it was no louder than normal speech.

For more than twenty years, the progress of my mother's disease had been slow—hardly noticeable, like the growth of a tree. More difficulty walking. Involuntary movements. Momentary hallucinations. She'd joke: "Dr. Parkinson isn't being his usual fun-loving self today."

Then the disease roared up like a bonfire. She graduated quickly from cane to walker to wheelchair to bed. Her limbs twisted. Her fine violinist's hands curled into claws, the skin taut and shiny.

But worst of all, the delusions. She started to believe people were stealing from her, destroying her belongings, and betraying her on every side. Once a creative, generous soul who drew friends the way a flower draws bees, she crumbled until little of her psyche was left but a sense of injury.

It's over now. I'm thankful Mom no longer struggles in a ruined body and a darkened mind.

Yet it's not over. My heart still aches over the torment she suffered. I wish I'd spent more time with her. I regret that I wasn't with her the night her life finally floated away like a wisp of smoke.

But there's a way I can strike back at Parkinson's disease. I can defy it—give it the finger—take back some of what it stole.

I can give to a nonprofit organization. They'll take my money, even a small amount, and fight Parkinson's disease. They'll help people who have it now. They'll fund research into better treatments. And maybe, someday, they'll find a cure—so Parkinson's can never take anyone else down that terrible road.

All it takes for me to move from defeat to victory is to give away some money. It's so easy.

It also works when I give to causes that were close to my mother's heart, like classical music or education. In fact—and here's the amazing part—I get the same positive effects no matter what causes I support, even those with no connection to her. It seems giving is giving. There are no pigeonholes, rankings, or limits.

Giving can't bring her back or erase the pain, but it re-orients me. I'm less a victim, more in control. Wiser, and less wounded.

My brush with Parkinson's disease isn't special or unusual. Everyone faces these things. You're in the same boat; if it hasn't happened yet, you or someone close to you will eventually fall under an attack of some kind, swift or slow, fatal or not. You'll take wounds so deep you'll wonder if you can survive.

But anyone can embrace the miracle of giving. It can ease your grief, revive your hope, and give you strength to face affliction, wrath, danger, and distress.

It's available whether you're wise or foolish, educated or ignorant, rich or poor, believer or nonbeliever. Giving is a light in darkness, a life vest in a storm, a song among tombs.

If you're a fundraiser, never forget the power you put in the hands of your donors when you present the opportunity to give. It's not just a monetary transaction.

And if you think you're taking something away from donors when you receive their gifts, you're missing the main point about what giving is and what it does.

I know fundraisers who are almost ashamed of their work. They equate it with begging or even scamming, as if they're getting the better of donors in some barely tolerable way. As if their only defense for getting money away from donors is the sad argument that the end justifies the means.

Anyone who feels that way simply isn't paying attention to what donors get in the deal.

Giving raises consciousness*

When you give to a cause, you immediately begin to care more about it. You pay more attention when it's in the news. It gets more concrete and important in your mind. That leads to other kinds of involvement—like volunteering, advocating, and spreading the word.

If you want to change the world in a meaningful way, I can't think of a better way to start than getting people to care with an act of charity as the first step. That's a lot more effective than trying to drum a new way of thinking into their unwilling heads.

---

* Most of the facts given on donors are taken from *Who Really Cares: America's Charity Divide*, by Arthur C. Brooks.

Beyond that, research shows that donors are dramatically more likely to commit all kinds of good deeds, like returning lost wallets, giving up their seat to older passengers on crowded buses, or giving blood. Donors are more kind, compassionate, and active than non-donors. When you ask them to give, you support their habit of virtue.

Giving creates happiness

Charitable giving stimulates the pleasure centers of the brain, the same way eating and sex do. Yes, giving is that primal. It's built into the core of our being. Part of what it is to be human is to freely give away some of what you have.

Social science research shows that donors are 43 percent more likely to say they're "very happy" than non-donors. This happiness comes from several sources:

▶ The well-documented "warm glow" of altruism that comes with the release of dopamine in the brain when people give.

▶ A more positive self-image. Donors see themselves as better people, as more in control. Donors can say, *"There's pain and chaos everywhere, but I can take a stand and do something about it!"* No doubt for the same reason, donors are generally perceived by themselves and by others as leaders.

▶ A sense of balance, because it's a way for people to give back some of what they've received. We all owe deep debts to the many people who have helped us through life. We can't possibly pay back those debts, but we can pay forward.

Giving improves health

Probably because of all these psychological benefits, giving also promotes physical health. Donors are 25 percent more likely to say their health is "excellent" or "very good" than non-donors.

Giving is financially beneficial

Here's the fact about giving that may surprise you: research shows that charitable giving has a return on investment of 3.75 to 1.

For every dollar given to charity, the donor eventually gets $3.75. Beat that in the stock market! A causal link is impossible to establish, but the correlation is clear: people who give to charity end up financially better off.

It's no get-rich-quick scheme, but it works. The ancients understood. Jesus Christ said, "Give, and it will be given to you: good measure, pressed down, shaken together, and running over" (Luke 6:38). St. Paul wrote (in a fundraising appeal, by the way) that *God loves a cheerful giver*. He believed givers acquire a special form of grace that lifts them to a higher plane.

*   *   *

Think for a moment about the impact charity has on society. Not just because of the important causes it funds, but because of the millions of healthier, happier, more involved donor-citizens it empowers. The whole world is better because of those donors and the way they live. If charitable giving weren't happening, our world would be darker and bleaker, more broken and brutal. More Hitlers would rise to power. Fewer Gandhis would emerge.

And fundraising is where it starts.

Sometimes I think we should remove our shoes or cover our heads while we work. Or compose hymns and anthems to sing while we work.

More often, though, I know it's good enough to go about our business the way everyone else goes about theirs. But deeply thankful that we're part of something so transforming and powerful—proud to be fundraisers.

About the Author

Jeff Brooks, creative director at TrueSense Marketing, has been serving the nonprofit community for more than 20 years, working as a copywriter and creative director on behalf of some of the best nonprofits of North America and Europe. His clients have included St. Jude Children's Research Hospital, CARE, The Salvation Army, Ronald McDonald House, World Vision, Feeding America, the American Cancer Society, and many more. He is deeply grateful to be part of an industry that makes the world a better place.

A leading advocate of donor-focused fundraising, Brooks champions that cause on his popular Future Fundraising Now blog (www.futurefundraisingnow.com) and the Fundraising Is Beautiful podcast (www.fundraisingisbeautiful.com), as a frequent contributor to *Fund-Raising Success* magazine, and as a frequent speaker at fundraising industry events.

In previous careers he has been a musician and an English teacher. He lives in Seattle, where from time to time the weather is spectacular.

Copies of this and other books from the publisher are available at discount when purchased in quantity for boards of directors or staff. Call 508-359-0019 or visit www.emersonandchurch.com

Emerson
& Church
PUBLISHERS

15 Brook Street • Medfield, MA 02052
Tel. 508-359-0019 • Fax 508-359-2703
www.emersonandchurch.com